Robert Anton Wilson

Beyond Conspiracy

Theory

RE/Search #18

ROBERT ANTON WILSON:
Beyond Conspiracy Theory
© 2019 RE/Search Publications
ISBN 978-1889307-28-2

PUBLISHERS/EDITORS: V. Vale, Marian Wallace
ASSISTANT EDITOR: Andrew Bishop

RE/Search copy editors, staff & consultants:

Seth Robson
Robert Collison
Yoshi Yubai

Photographs are by V. Vale and RE/Search unless otherwise noted. Every effort has been made to trace the copyright holders and obtain permission to reproduce this material.

*Please check our website or contact us to find
out about our full line of books and media.*

RE/Search Publications
20 Romolo Place #B
San Francisco, CA 94133
(415) 362-1465
info@researchpubs.com
www.researchpubs.com

TABLE OF CONTENTS

Editor's note

V. Vale interviewed Robert Anton Wilson in San Francisco on Friday, August 30, 1985. The interview was intended to be the centerpiece of a proposed RE/Search special issue dedicated to Wilson, modeled on *RE/Search #8/9: J.G. Ballard*.

Wilson also submitted many supporting documents (along with permission to print them), which were intended to complement the interview and represent the varied aspects of his work.

The project was intended to include:

- A transcript of Robert Anton Wilson's talk 'Whatever You Say You Are, You Aren't' (recorded by Vale in San Francisco a few hours after the interview)
- An interview with Sean McBride, conducted by Robert Anton Wilson
- Several poems by Robert Anton Wilson
- Excepts from *The New Inquisition*
- An essay titled 'The New Physics and Carl Jung' (which appeared in German in *Psychologie Heute*, but which has never been published in English)
- Discordian collages by Greg Hill and Robert Anton Wilson
- A list of books from Wilson's library

- An International Conspiracy Trivia Quiz (which Wilson re-wrote specifically for RE/Search)

The RE/Search issue was never completed. Wilson later integrated parts of the RE/Search project into his book *Coincidance: A Head Test* (1988). The collaboration was confined to the RE/Search archives until it was rediscovered in 2016.

In preparing the present volume, the editors decided to omit most of the historical material provided by Robert Anton Wilson. Since 1985, Wilson has become a well-known and influential figure in global counterculture. A general introduction to Wilson as a thinker and writer no longer seems necessary.

We are also very pleased to see that Robert Anton Wilson's books (including *Coincidance*) are being brought back into print by Hilaritas Press (*www.hilaritaspress. com*).

Instead, we took the opportunity to present an inspiring, more focused volume in which Wilson addresses many of the most pressing issues affecting us today. This book might be the nearest you'll get to Wilson's take on Trump's America—a world in which conspiracy theory has become mainstream.

Introduction by Andrew Bishop

Like many others, I first read Robert Anton Wilson in my early 20s as part of a *search for weirdness*. I had grown up watching *The X-Files*, and I was eager for more mysterious, conspiracy-themed entertainment. When I finally picked up *Cosmic Trigger*, I found that Wilson delivers much more than weirdness. His books intend to upgrade the reader's brain "software", just as computer software is upgradable.

Wilson's recounting of his own initiatory experiences in *Cosmic Trigger* blew my mind—but not in a flashy, explosive way. Instead, Wilson subtly destabilized my unconscious habits of thought and language. He invited me to remain in a permanent state of questioning wonder.

What impressed me most about Wilson's writing was that he didn't seem to draw any *conclusions* at all. He went deep into psychology, philosophy, politics, and conspiracy theory, but came out the other side not "believing" anything. Rather than picking a side, Wilson nudges his readers into "model agnosticism" (a term from physics which holds that any explanation of the world is only a model, and should not be confused with the world itself). Between the extremes of belief and incredulity, Wilson reveals a whole spectrum of "maybe".

Seeing the world as a spectrum of "maybe" came very easily after reading Wilson. His "maybe logic" gradually takes hold like a viral infection, erasing all trace of dogmatism and certainty. Rather than being *either* true or false, facts now existed along a continuum of possibility. This way of operating in the world was a lot of fun as well as a great stress reliever!

Through his fiction, and his how-to manuals such as *Prometheus Rising*, Wilson embarked on a mission to upgrade our mental operating systems to a "quantum psychology" based on Korzybski's General Semantics. And with a mischievous sense of humor, he made Korzybski more easily palatable. Thanks to Wilson, I began to naturally pick up habits of thought and language inspired by General Semantics. Never again was something "bad"—at most, it "seemed 'bad' to me, at this time, on this date".

Another shock to my system was Wilson's idea that scientific materialism could be fundamentalist. Wilson's "model agnosticism" refuses total belief in anything, and is against all forms of fundamentalism—including models accepted on faith by the scientific community. Having grown up in the U.K., where anything suggested by an apparently "scientific" study or theory tends to be automatically accepted as true, I may never have recognized this error in judgment without Wilson's laughing guidance.

Wilson's high hopes for our technological future may appear naïve to a new reader. In this 1985 interview, Wilson claimed that space colonies were mere years away, that we would soon eradicate world hunger, and that longevity (if not immortality) was imminent. Wilson's predictions are best not evaluated for their "accuracy". In this interview, he acknowledges that as a technological seer he has room for improvement. Instead, Wilson's predictions are best understood as an expression of his deliberately nurtured *optimism*. Some of Wilson's technological predictions may look absurd 35 years later—but his demonstration of optimism, of having a "winner script", still applies. As Wilson says, "If you think you can't get the job, you're not going in for the interview."

Wilson specialized in conspiracy theory, which during his lifetime was mostly confined to the lunatic fringes of human thought. But our world has changed dramatically since this 1985 interview. In the age of President Trump, conspiracy theory has been popularized, and it seems like we are living in Robert Anton Wilson's world.

Take, for example, Wilson's concept of the "reality tunnel". Wilson explained that we filter out information that doesn't fit our existing belief system (which Wilson abbreviates as "B.S."!), focusing only on information that is congruent with our basic expectations. If we are honest, we will admit that we have no idea what is (or isn't) true. All we can "know" is which bits of information got through our filters.

Facebook, the platform on which most humans now get their news, exploits our "reality tunnels" in the same way. Facebook typically only shows us what fits our particular filter bubble, our existing preferences and reality tunnels. Any content that will release a little bit of *dopamine* is okay by Facebook—regardless of its "truthfulness". This digital implementation of the *confirmation bias* can be hijacked by bad actors such as Cambridge Analytica, which employed Facebook's mastery over our reality tunnels to reinvent and automate voter suppression and electoral persuasion.

What would once have been considered the crazed ramblings of conspiracy nuts is now mainstream political opinion. Vaccines cause autism, mass shootings are staged, 9/11 was an inside job, and the government controls the weather. In short, Operation Mindfuck (as depicted in *Illuminatus!*) has taken over contemporary

Photo: Yoshi Yubai

culture. Wilson used conspiracy theory to expose the pernicious traps in our thinking, nudging us to question our fundamental assumptions. In 2019, Wilson's "model agnosticism" seems more necessary than ever. If he were alive today, Wilson would be among the few remaining voices of clarity.

And, if you're wondering what Robert Anton Wilson might say about President Donald Trump in 2019, he already said it on Dutch television in 1999, even deploying a rarely-used 'is' of identity: "Donald Trump is fucking crazy."

Robert Anton Wilson immersed himself in conspiracy theory, and yet he managed to remain both optimistic and agnostic about everything to the end. For Wilson, optimism is a choice—another upgrade to the brain's software. As inhabitants of Wilson's future, we'll be lucky to maintain such levels of optimism and discernment.

—Andrew Bishop, April 2019
(*www.andrew-bishop.com*)

◆ ◆ ◆

An interview with
ROBERT ANTON WILSON

V. Vale interviewed Robert Anton Wilson in San Francisco on Friday August 30, 1985. That evening, Wilson was to give a lecture at the Unitarian Center (on Franklin & Geary) titled 'Whatever You Say You Are, You Aren't'.

I live in Ireland in a little village called Howth. It's mostly fishermen and their families, and a few writers and artists from Dublin who have come for the peace and quiet. I feel I'm in a little *timeless* zone, where my creativity can flow freely. But I also spend three months of the year traveling, so I get to meet exciting, interesting people.

I went to L.A. and ran into people coming up with new technologies. Like, I just heard holophonic sound demonstrated—that's going to make stereo obsolete! It's so much better.

Then I stopped by Silicon Gulch to hear what the latest thing is in the computer business. In Boulder, I had a fascinating brainwave experiment done on me. I go to Amsterdam twice a year, and so on.

I go here and there, so I manage to keep in touch with what's going on. At the same time I have this little timeless zone where I retreat to do my writings. A nice way of life!

What's the L5 Society?

The L5 Society, which I *used to* belong to—

"Used to"?

Yeah. I got tired of the politics. I got pissed off about the political divisions within the L5 Society. So I said, "Let *them* fight it out among themselves," and I just dropped out.

There's a big split between the right wing and the left wing of the L5 Society. Meanwhile, I feel things are moving along just as fast as they should move. NASA *does* have the technology right now to put up small space colonies. It's just a matter of years before the public becomes excited and curious—the idea has gotten enough publicity.

I think very shortly they will start; they can put up colonies for a hundred people *right now*. But they don't have the authorization to do it yet! I feel we're getting closer all the time. A lot of people are turned on by the idea, but a lot of people are turned off *right away*—I find that amusing.

Really?

Oh yes, some people *hate* it! Well, there were people who disapproved of the industrial revolution. There were people standing around when the Wright brothers took off, saying, "You'll never get *me* up in one of those! I told Wilbur and I told Orville, you're going to come down with a hell of a crash!"

So the L5 Society is dedicated to getting people up in space?

To propagandizing for that idea. But then they fight about the military uses of space. I'm all against the military uses of space, but I didn't want to get involved in the infighting—it seemed too silly to me. Everybody was too bigoted, all around.

That's what always happens to organizations—

Yes, they always split. I think it's a natural evolutionary development: organizations *should* split! But it seems people are still operating on these old primate circuits, and they can't split without having to fight first. They've got to denounce one another, and so on.

A cell doesn't have a fight before it splits off into two cells—

Exactly. Groups should grow to a certain size and then split. But first, they've got to have an ideological fight over it. And if it's the Middle East, sometimes they've got to get guns and shoot each other for a while.

So even though, in a sense, your presence is kind of a threat to certain powers that be, you're not at all *personally* paranoid?

No. I don't know why.

You don't know why? Maybe humor is your natural defense.

Yeah, well, some people seem prone to paranoia, others seem strangely immune to it. I've been in lots of paranoid situations. Not only the peace movement in Chicago [1968], but I was involved in the Timothy Leary Defense Committee back in the early seventies. Boy, was *that* a hotbed of paranoia!

Was Joanna Harcourt-Smith [Leary's companion] an agent?

I don't know. I wouldn't even begin to guess. All I can say is: she's one of the most remarkable human beings I've ever met… and I can't figure her out. I like her; I basically trust her up to a point. But I don't know.

That Leary Defense Committee was a great education in paranoia! Everybody in the committee (at one point or another) suspected everybody else of being a government agent!

I was suspected by quite a few people; I'm pretty sure Allen Ginsberg suspected me for a while. Somehow I went through the whole thing assuming that some people were government agents and some weren't… but what *I'm* doing is within the law.

Of course, people do get framed, and so on. I just feel that if you're going to get involved in controversy, you're taking risks. And you should accept that without getting neurotic about it—especially if you're defending unpopular causes.

I've been involved in many controversial causes, and the worst thing that happened was in Seattle when I got hit with a pie! And that scared the hell out of me. I'm immune to paranoia, but not to *anxiety*. When this guy came at me with the pie, I saw him out of the corner of my eye and thought it was a knife. But, how can you confuse a *pie* with a *knife*?

Well, that shows what happens when you're being attacked. People who are shot often can't give an accurate description of the gunman to the police, because you go into the emergency circuits in the brain and your perceptions aren't very accurate. I saw this metal thing this guy was raising and I remembered Martin Luther King being stabbed. That was *before* King was shot—he was stabbed at a book signing many years earlier.

Wow, I never knew that!

I also thought of John Lennon. It's been open season on politicians since the early sixties, and after Lennon, I felt it's open season on artists, too. I was really scared for a second, and then when I got hit with a pie I was so *relieved!*

Oh, god. Were you mad?

Yeah, because I felt he had scared me. Before, I had always thought throwing pies was funny, like in Laurel and Hardy. But when he scared me, I thought, "Gee, this isn't funny at *all!* He has no idea what he did to my glands and my heart, and so on."

How did you react?

What I said to the audience was, "Isn't it a shame when cousins marry?"

Did you ever read a book called *Alternative 3*?

That's the one about the secret colony on the moon. Well, that's an example of what I mean about conspiracy books being full of uncritical thinking. I can't prove that the book *isn't* true. But the evidence presented is far from convincing. The best you can say for it is that it's *mildly plausible*—and I don't even find it mildly plausible!

But I've read a lot of books like that. Since *The Illuminatus! Trilogy* came out, people keep sending me crackpot books. Some are sent to "convert" me, but most of them say, "I think you'll find this amusing." I've gotten all sorts of crackpot books and pamphlets, and I know more "alternative realities" than practically anyone else on this planet!

I get books about the Hollow Earth. I got a book recently that claims that not only is the Earth hollow, but Jules Verne knew about it… and Jules Verne was actually an initiate of the Bavarian Illuminati. Fascinating stuff.

Next question!

What's one of the most annoying, recurring uses of language that you've encountered in media like *Time* or the *New York Times*?

"Is". The "is" of identity, as in "Beethoven is better than Mozart." Or "Mozart is better than Beethoven." Or "Picasso is a better artist than Van Gogh." Or "This is a dirty movie." Or "This is a sexist book." Or "This is Communism." I agree with Count Korzybski, the inventor of General Semantics, that all those statements imply a metaphysics that is now known to be scientifically obsolete.

All of those statements should be reformulated as "*seems to me*". "Beethoven *seems to me* better than Mozart." "Picasso *seems to me* better than Van Gogh." "This *seems to me* a sexist movie."

That's more accurate, yeah.

I find it hilarious that educated people will sit around and argue about things like that. "No, Beethoven *really is* better!" "No, you idiot, Mozart is better!" All they're talking about is how their nervous systems are functioning.

The universe does not come with labels. Anything you put a label on, *you're* putting the label on. That's the essence of Nietzsche and his whole rebellion against "good and evil." Things do not have labels on them saying "good" and "evil"—that's always a human judgment. That doesn't mean that we don't have to *make* such judgments—that is part of the human "trip." But we've got to realize *we're* making the judgment.

Things just do not come with labels on them. *Behind the Green Door*—if you hung a label on it saying "sexist", *you* would still be the one hanging the label on it! I'm astonished that educated people don't understand that. Educated people are frequently as ignorant as uneducated people in many ways. We just don't have an adequate educational system, yet.

People get into fights over "is". People sometimes shoot each other over "is". How many people were killed in Germany because of the statement "He is a Jew" or "She is a Jew"? Nobody is a "Jew". A "Jew" is a label which means different things to different people putting the labels on.

Do you think there actually is evil in the world?

No, there is no evil in the world. "Evil" is a word used by human beings to describe various things that they find obnoxious. I find many things obnoxious, myself. I find the bombing of civilian populations obnoxious, so I call it "evil". But I'm aware that that's *my judgment*. In the world there is no good, no evil. No up, no down. No true, no false. The world comes without labels.

There's a Zen riddle that puts this very clearly: "Who is the master who makes the grass green?" Once you know the master who makes the grass green, then you know who creates good and evil and who decides what's progressive and what's taboo.

A lot of people take Hitler as the incarnation of evil.

I take Hitler as the incarnation of certain evolutionary trends which *appear very evil to me*. This is a very hard point and most people can't accept it at all. **But the world is not a word.** People are not words, events are not words.

You asked me what linguistics I find most pernicious. I started with "is". The "either/or" habit is very pernicious. It *seems very pernicious to me*, I mean. Two-valued situations are relatively rare, actually. It's just a habit of Western culture to try to make everything fit into either A or not-A. University usually gives you five or six choices, or a couple of million sometimes. Either/or is the foundation of a lot of stupid politics. "This is either true Americanism or it's some kind of foreign deviation." All over Europe people ask me, "Why don't they have socialized medicine in the United States yet?" Well, because of either/or logic!

"Everything is either capitalist or socialist. Socialized medicine is socialist, therefore it's wrong." And you know, meanwhile we've got the Canadians just across the border who have had it for years—it hasn't destroyed their society! Everybody in Europe has it, and so on. But this either/or thinking just continues to control people astoundingly.

That's another reason I live in Ireland: Ireland has quasi-socialized medicine. We've got to pay for it, but it's much cheaper than the voluntary health plan we could get in America. My wife recently spent two weeks in hospital. After the government was through paying their share we owed a couple of hundred dollars. In this country I would have owed $15,000 or $30,000—I don't know what! I'd be in debt for the next ten years! I think it takes a lot of courage to live in America.

Really?

Yeah, it takes a lot of courage and a lot of faith that you're never going to have a serious illness.

Or a lot of insurance.

For freelancers like myself, if you're not working for a corporation to get enough insurance, it's more of a burden than most people can carry. Most self-employed people just have a moderate amount of insurance, with high hopes nothing really *serious* will happen.

You never had anything serious happen, like being in jail in this country?

I was arrested once for trespassing... I'm a dangerous international trespasser!

That was in Yellow Springs, Ohio in 1962. A bunch of students had done a sit-in at a local barbershop, protesting against segregation. Then a bunch of us adults decided there should be more of an *adult* protest so people couldn't say, "Ah, it's just a bunch of radical students!"

We consulted a lawyer who told us the horrible truth that the previous student-sit-in had triggered a *court injunction* against further sit-ins. So, because of this injunction, a sit-in became "contempt of court"— meaning: now the judge can hit you with anything he wants. So our group shrank from twenty to about six overnight! And I'll tell you the truth—*I* lost my nerve the morning of the sit-in. I said, "I can't do this, I don't want to go to jail for an indeterminate period."

That and similar experiences are behind the theme that appears in a couple of my books: **Courage is something you never totally own or totally lose.** Because by the time the hour came, I went inside the barbershop, in spite of being scared stiff for a few hours earlier. And it turned out that they didn't invoke contempt of court against us! They just arrested us for trespassing. But the case never came to court. The barber sold the barbershop, moved further south, and opened another segregated barbershop in Kentucky.

That's my only experience like that. I was in a police station for a couple of hours before bail was made. They took my picture and gave me a number.

What do you think of political activity today?

I think radical political activity has become a lot more intelligent. I think the people who are still trying to carry on like the sixties are not very effective and not very smart. I think Bob Geldof, for instance, is a lot more intelligent. I think there's just as much utopianism around as there was in the sixties, and just as much creative energy, but it's expressing itself in more intelligent forms. People have gotten a lot shrewder about where the levers are that can actually change things. The either/or thing, a lot of people have seen through. I think one of the big mistakes of the sixties—and Abbie Hoffman was the most notorious example of this—was: antagonizing everybody instead of trying to convert or persuade them.

I mean, a lot of people in the sixties were just into it for an ego trip: "Look how moral I am, and look how immoral the rest of you are." That never gets you anywhere. It may be very soothing to the ego and a lot of fun perhaps, but it doesn't accomplish a damn thing.

In spite of the continuation of terrorism in the world, I think it's becoming obvious that terrorism is counterproductive. I think it always plays into the hands of the reactionary forces. That's why "they" do it so often themselves, like P2 was doing in Italy. They were creating more terrorism than actually existed!

How did you find out about the P2?

There are two good books that will tell you a great deal about P2: *In God's Name* by David Yallop and *In Banks We Trust* by Penny Lernoux. Penny Lernoux's book is better in many ways—it's better documented. Yallop I'm not sure of. A lot of his sources are confidential and when people are quoting confidential sources it becomes a matter of judgment—how much one is willing to trust them. But if you put the two books together, you'll see that a lot of Yallop can be documented from other sources. Not *everything* in Yallop, but a great deal. Mostly I've been clipping things out of newspapers for the last three years.

You keep scrapbooks?

Yeah. I've been saving stuff about P2 because I got interested right away. It was so much like one of my novels that I wanted to know more about it!

I was interviewed on a San Diego radio station and I started talking about P2 and their infiltration of the Vatican Bank. This was on tape. As soon as we were finished, the interviewer told me they were going to have to cut out the stuff about the Vatican Bank. Which they did—it never went over the air.

I find it fascinating when they're that upfront about it! He could have said nothing to me and then after it was

cut, if I wrote him a letter, he could have said, "Well, we didn't have time for everything." You run into a lot of that kind of evasion. But he was absolutely upfront about it: "We can't let you say things like that about the Vatican— there are too many Catholics in San Diego."

Have you ever been to Egypt?

No, I haven't yet. I'd like to.

What do you talk about in your lecture on *Finnegans Wake* and the *I Ching*?

I really need a blackboard and a couple of hours. I just did a 10-hour seminar on that at Esalen Institute and I think that was clearer than any of the two-hour lectures I've given on it. I think it really *does* take about 10 hours to explain all that. I've done it as a two-hour lecture a few times.

Some people show signs of enlightenment in the audience, but some of them show signs of acute consternation. Trying to put it into a short answer is hopeless.

Are you ever going to write it?

Oh, yeah. I've got 300 pages of a book on that written [some of this material was worked into 1988's *Coincidance: A Head Test*]. I'm not ready to submit that anywhere because I haven't quite got it in the right order. I think the Esalen seminar helped a lot, and the book will follow the order of the seminar. I think I found the right order, finally, to present the ideas.

Do you use your dreams much?

Yes.

Do you keep a dream journal?

Not lately. I did for many years and then I just felt like I've been doing that long enough. Maybe I'll get back to it someday. There are some things you do for years and then you decide, "Well, that's enough of that." Then sometimes you figure, "Well, I've got to start it over again—I'm missing something." Right now I'm not keeping a dream journal. But I did for years—many things in my novels come out of my dreams.

I think if you keep a record of your dreams, it starts a conversation between the two hemispheres of your brain. Then your dreams get more left-brain feedback. This is a guess, but I think dreams come from the right hemisphere. And if you keep records of them, then your left-brain thinks about them. Then when you dream again, the right-brain has gotten feedback during the day. This is just a guess, although there's some evidence for it. I think the right-brain knows everything the left-brain is doing, but the left-brain generally doesn't pay attention to the right-brain. The left-brain is digital-analytical and the right-brain is analogical-holistic, roughly speaking.

These are oversimplifications—everybody in neurology these days is backing away from that; they think the differences are oversimplified. I'll stand by my statement, with the addition that it's *slightly* oversimplified. There's also a polarity between the front and the back. The back brain has got the more primitive circuits; the front brain has the later circuits. So you really need a four-fold division to describe the brain.

The frontal lobes are the latest circuits. I suspect that's the location of what Leary calls the higher circuits. The back brain is very definitely the lower circuits—they are directly connected to the body—

Motor functions?

—the motor functions and muscular reactions and so on. The most primitive circuit is the one that you feel all over your body at once. That's the one that has to do with safety and danger. That's probably the earliest, in terms of evolution. That's why if you're scared, it's not an intellectual process at all. You feel it all over the body at once (and if you have chronic anxiety, you get ulcers!). That circuit is very, very far back in the old brain, directly connected with the autonomic nervous system and the glandular systems and so on. And the frontal lobes seem to be very, very independent of the body. One theory about ketamine is that it turns off everything but the front lobes, so you don't have any emotions or body sensations.

What's ketamine?

Ketamine is a drug that's been researched by John Lilly and others. It produces a unique kind of consciousness which seems disembodied or non-local. It seems even closer than LSD to descriptions of "mystical experience." That very well may be because the frontal lobes just don't pay any attention to emotions or body feelings, so you're in a totally mental space—you're not in physical body space. At least that's *my* guess about how ketamine works.

Have you tried it?

Yes, under medical supervision. I would not recommend anybody try it without medical supervision. Seriously— with a heavy dose of ketamine, I'm pretty sure that if the house were on fire, you would not get up and walk out! So you really need somebody supervising it, and it should be a *medical* person to make sure there's no overdose. I don't encourage casual experimentation with ketamine by any means.

Or with any drug?

Or with any drug.

Do you feel logical and rational on ketamine?

It's a combination. You can be very logical on ketamine, but you're also aware of a lot that logic isn't usually aware of. It seems to be a very holistic form of consciousness. Very holistic and very, very detached. John Lilly calls it "consciousness without an object," or something like that. You feel very much like Hegel's definition of "absolute being."

Jeez.

I can't remember Hegel's definition! I just read Bertrand Russell's parody of it. His parody of Hegel's concept of absolute being is "pure thought thinking about pure thought". And that's sort of what ketamine is like: pure thought thinking about pure thought.

How much value do you think one can get from drug experiences? How much value did you get out of this experience?

I think what you get depends on the drug. I don't think cocaine has done any good for anybody I've ever seen. I can't see any improvement in people who take cocaine—I see signs of disimprovement. That's a popular word in England these days—do they use it in this country at all yet?

No! That's good!

I see a lot of signs of this "disimprovement"!
So it depends on the drug. What you get out of

psychedelics like LSD and psilocybin—I agree with Tim Leary—it depends on the dosage, the set, and the setting. The set means your philosophical epistemological set— how you go into it, what you're expecting to get out of it. If you're doing it for casual entertainment, you may scare the hell out of yourself because you're not prepared for all the things you're going to meet. If you go into it in a religious or psychotherapeutic setting, expecting to expand your consciousness and get new insight, you probably will. But it also depends on the setting. I think the setting should be natural and homey. It should be someplace in the woods near a stream, and nobody should be wearing laboratory smocks and acting like scientists. The experimenter should be dressed casually! You don't want to create a laboratory feeling it all—it tends to induce paranoia. I definitely do *not* encourage the use of psychedelics for recreation.

Have you ever read Stanislav Grof?

Yes, I think Grof pretty much comes to the same conclusions as Leary. He uses a different language but I think he would agree with what I just said. I think it's a terrible tragedy that this research has been stopped. They stopped the research because they were afraid of recreational use. So the result is: the research has been stopped, but the recreational use still goes on! That seems to be counterproductive, somehow.

And I think it's a shame that they've made ecstasy illegal. A lot of psychiatrists thought they were getting very good results with that. But now, because of all the publicity, they can't use it. Of course, it's appearing on the black market—or something under that name is appearing on the black market. God knows what it is.

Sometimes, it seems the government never forgets anything, and never learns anything.

What did you learn from visiting Silicon Valley?

Well, you can find a lot of people talking about designing software that will be both appealing and fun, and incompatible with authoritarian educational systems. The software will in itself force the school system to modify in a more humanistic direction than it traditionally had. I like to hear people talking who are actually in the business and will be able to put their ideas into practice. That's what I meant about revolutionaries becoming more intelligent. I hear a lot of things like that.

There are also a lot of people in show business who are very aware of their power and want to use it in good ways. I mean, you might call that The Bob Geldof Phenomenon. There are a lot of people who haven't done anything as big as Geldof, but are thinking along the same lines: "We've got all this power; we should use it in beneficial ways." And then the next thought, as they're pretty bright people: "We've got to think carefully so we don't fuck up." They're really trying to be not only progressive but intelligent, and I find that a very hopeful sign.

I think what Geldof did was absolutely stupendous. It really worked. It not only raised a lot of money but it got the message across that we *can* abolish starvation, which the Hunger Project has been trying to get across for 10 years. I think he did more in one night than they did in 10 years. Not putting them down at all—Geldof just came at the right time and saw the opportunity. He probably wouldn't have done it if there hadn't been 10 years' preparation. Actually, that was 30 years' preparation— Bucky Fuller was saying back in the fifties that it would be possible to abolish starvation.

Did you ever know him?

Yeah. I met him several times. I admired him tremendously.

I used to like him a lot.

I think he has more successful predictions to his credit than any other futurist. So I keep rereading his books, trying to internalize more of his method of thinking... because I would like some of *my* predictions to be correct, too!

What *are* some of your predictions?

I think we're going to have space colonies within 10 years. I don't know how *big* a breakthrough the first one will be, but... some kind of breakthrough will happen. There's so much research going on that somebody is going to hit on the right approach pretty soon. Statistically, it's bound to happen.

People are approaching longevity from so many different angles, with so many different research teams. Somebody is going to hit on something important soon. And I think starvation will be abolished in the next 10 years. That's right on schedule—Fuller said that by 1995 starvation would be abolished, and it's getting more and more obvious that Fuller was on target.

What evidence do you have that starvation will be abolished?

Well, the fact that so many people *did* contribute to Live Aid. So many people looked at that and got the message. And the fact that the modern media makes it impossible to ignore things like that. Fifty years ago starvation could have raged across a couple of continents and nobody in the United States would have thought about it or even heard much about it. But now television brings it right into your living room. Fuller said that the 1960s would be an age of radical activity because the first generation of television children would be coming of age, and they would have more information than their parents. More and *later* information, so they would see that there's something wrong with society and would try to change it.

But he said the *big* change will come in the 1980s when you get the second generation of television children, and I think Geldof is one of them.

I think the whole world is going to change more for the next 30 years than it has in the last 6,000. I don't know in what ways—I can just dimly discern some of them, like longevity, and the abolition of starvation, and more and more people going into space. I don't know what comes after that because there are so many possibilities. But the one thing I do feel sure about is that the changes will be *accelerating*. They'll be happening faster and faster and they'll be increasingly dramatic. That's based on the fact that knowledge is doubling faster all the time, and the lag between knowledge and the *application of knowledge* is getting shorter all the time, too.

Between 1500 and 1900, knowledge doubled twice. And if you look at the world of 1500 and the world of 1900 you can see the tremendous change that had occurred. But since 1900, knowledge has doubled about eight times. It doubled between 1900 and 1950, and again it doubled by 1960, and again it doubled by 1967. It's doubling faster all the time.

It's strictly impossible to predict the number of breakthroughs that are coming up, but you can say there will be more change than ever before. Which means that the **reactionaries are going to get shriller and more paranoid**—they always do in times of change. So instead of denouncing rock 'n' roll or fluoridation as a communist plot, they'll be getting paranoid about more and more things. Reactionaries are basically terrified of change, and they're going to be getting more and more of it.

Since we don't know what "reality" is anymore, and since the universe is a puzzle, every statement you make is a statement about yourself to some extent. That derives from what I was saying earlier about quantum mechanics. You separate the observer from the observed—you can only make models that describe how our minds analyze things. It comes up from every branch of psychology—existential therapy, gestalt therapy, perception theory, neurological psychology. No matter where you look, you find more and more evidence that the observer and the observed cannot be sharply separated in the old way. So we're always talking about ourselves.

And there is such a thing as a self-fulfilling prophecy. Nobody knows which prophecies are self-fulfilling, but if you think you can't pass the examination you're not going to study. If you think you can't get the job you're not going in for the interview. So on those grounds, I think that professional pessimists are really talking about themselves. They're saying, "*I* feel powerless, *I* feel helpless, and *you* should feel powerless and helpless, too."

On the other hand, optimism often does work as a self-fulfilling prophecy, too. Sometimes it's faintly nefarious. I worked once as a salesman when I was very young. They used to have sales meetings where they would use classic brainwashing techniques to convince us all that out there were millions of people dying to buy our product and we just had to find them and get the message across. If they didn't seem to want it, it was because we hadn't radiated enough positive energy yet! I understand brainwashing from the *inside.* That's faintly nefarious but it works. When sales departments train their salesmen that way, they do go out and sell a hell of a lot. (Sometimes they sell a hell of a lot of *junk.*)

I think the higher you raise up human aspirations and expectations, the more good results you are going to get. That's why I frequently supported the immortalist movement. This is a bunch of scientists and science groupies who say, "Why aim for longevity? Let's aim for immortality!"

I really don't know how reasonable that is. But I

think it's worth bringing the idea up just because: the higher you aim, the more you'll achieve. I know a couple of researchers—and these people are not "nuts" by any means, they're quite intelligent people. They were aiming for immortality. And my feeling is: "Good for them—if they don't get there, they'll undoubtedly find longevity while they're trying to get to immortality."

So I'm all for raising expectations and aspirations. The revolution of lowered expectations which we were hearing so much about in the seventies seemed to me the

most dangerous idea of the 20th century—while people were starving, while the Cold War was still going on. When the world is in such a mess, to tell people "Lower your expectations! Things are only going to get worse from here on!" I think that was absolutely pernicious and nefarious. I was going around telling people, "Raise your expectations! Demand more!" As the French student revolution [May, 1968] said: "Think of your desires as realities."

Yes!

To me, you've got this basic choice: optimism or pessimism. It comes down to transactional analysis. Do you have a winner script or a loser script? And people who want a loser script, that's okay with me—they can go blow their brains out with the Saturday Night Special any time they want. But I don't think they're going to accomplish anything. People with winner scripts usually accomplish something. I noticed down in Silicon Valley that companies are *not* started by people who think they're *not* going to make a lot of money!

Hmm. We underestimate what is possible.

And also we're stronger than we think we are. A lot of pessimism comes from inadequate self-knowledge. We're all stronger and tougher than we think... People, in this society especially, are too afraid of pain, too afraid of suffering. They think it will destroy them. Actually, it doesn't—as Nietzsche said, *anything that doesn't destroy me makes me stronger.* I think if people understand that better, they'd be much more optimistic. That's the one time I felt something in common with G. Gordon Liddy.

Oh, his book *Will* was really amazing—

I haven't read that, but when he got out of prison I saw his first interview. He's coming out of the prison and reporters are all around him asking questions. He's saying "No comment, no comment, no comment." And one of the reporters says: "Do you have anything to say about the prison system?" And Gordon Liddy turned around and said: "Anything that doesn't kill me makes me stronger." I suddenly thought G. Gordon Liddy and I have something in common—we both like that quote from Nietzsche!

Apropos of my fondness for Nietzsche and Gordon Liddy... I'm not *really* fond of Gordon Liddy! Somebody was trying to sell an interview with me to the *Bay Guardian*, and the editor rejected it on the grounds that I'm a Satanist. I was really delighted with that. I think it's such a perfect illustration of what I'm talking about in my lecture tonight—the 'is' of identity. I don't know how the hell he got that label to pin on me.

Do you think he confused you with Anton LaVey?! [laughter]

I've been called a lot of things, but being called a "Satanist" was so new and original.

But why would he call you a Satanist?!

It just goes to show that people will pin any damn label on any damn thing! Maybe he got me mixed up with Anton LaVey, or maybe he tried to read one of my books once and that was the best label he could find for it!

What do you think about the cults of people who have read your books and not seen the ironic humor or the puzzle?

The only Illuminati cult I know is the Illuminatus Nut

Cult that's founded by a fellow named Arthur Hlavaty. The Illuminatus Nut Cult is just a group of fans of my books. They call themselves a "nut cult"—that's just one of Arthur's jokes. They certainly don't take me very seriously, or regard me as a guru or anything like that. A few of them have shown signs of that, but I have managed to scare the hell out of them and they dropped out. I don't want people treating me as a guru or anything like that. It's a dangerous position to get caught in. It's the quickest path to megalomania, or worse. I have my ways of discouraging that attitude. [laughter]

I've been influenced by certain obscure books like *Against Nature* by Huysmans, for example. The aphorisms of Nietzsche, too. How about yourself? Have there been key books that you would mention?

Very definitely. There's a long list. I think among the books that had the biggest influence on me were several books by Nietzsche: *Twilight of the Idols* and *The Anti-Christ*. Nietzsche, in general, has had a tremendous impact on me—his whole attack on grammar and the way language controls thought. There is no good and evil in the universe, and "The Leaf" does not exist—all that exists is this leaf and that leaf and the other leaf, but nobody has ever seen "The Leaf". The whole epistemological radicalism. Nietzsche was sort of the forerunner of 20th-century linguistic analysis, in one dimension—his whole criticism of conventional morality.

And another major influence is somebody that hardly anyone has heard of. Whenever I run into somebody who's heard of Benjamin Tucker, I'm astonished. Very few people have read Ben Tucker. Strangely, two of my favorite novelists read him and mentioned him: Henry Miller and James Joyce both read Ben Tucker. I don't know who else has ever read Ben Tucker. He wrote one book in his whole lifetime—it's called *Instead of a Book, by a Man Too Busy to Write One*. It's a fantastically logical book.

I don't always trust logic—I know how many traps there are in logic—but it's one of the most beautifully logical books I've ever read. And it's a rebuttal to every form of philosophy that claims that somebody should have authority over somebody else. Tucker called himself an 'individualist anarchist,' or sometimes he changed it to 'philosophical anarchist,' to mean he wasn't in favor of violence and bombing things and so on. But it's the best defense of the rights of the individual I have ever read, and it has had a tremendous influence on me.

And then, Joyce's experiments with language in *Ulysses* and *Finnegans Wake*. And Korzybski's *Science and Sanity*, which encouraged me in my Joycean tendency to suspect that language is full of traps and **it's the job of the writer to find his way around the traps in language and not just fall into them**. I think there are two types of writers—those who are aware of the traps in language and try to avoid them—not always successfully. We're not all geniuses, we make mistakes. And the second type is those who aren't aware of the traps and fall into them on one page after another. Tucker was aware of that too—the traps in language. So Nietzsche, Tucker, Joyce, and Korzybski have all influenced me to look at language in a peculiar way. **I see language as a means of human liberation, potentially—and the main mechanism of human slavery** most of the time. It depends on how you use language.

Who else has influenced me as much as those? Andrew Dixon White's *A History of the Warfare of Science with Theology in Christendom* had a big influence on me, and probably still does. I've got a permanent suspicion of all theological and metaphysical language.

Bertrand Russell, in many ways, has been a big influence on me. I trust Russell more than most philosophers. I don't always *agree* with him, but I have a basic feeling that he was trying to be clear and he was trying to be honest. A lot of philosophers I feel I don't quite trust, or trust their language.

Raymond Chandler convinced me that there were possibilities of poetry and humor in American speech that nobody else had discovered. I feel every book I write is a tribute to Chandler. It may not be obvious on the surface—I use different tricks than him. Although... I use a lot of his tricks, too, at times! But I'm always trying to do what Chandler did—to write what looks like natural American speech, but has the qualities of humor and poetry. Chandler taught me how to do that. Chandler is vastly admired in France and England, but in this country is still regarded as just a detective-story writer.

It's pathetic. Well, he's being looked at more, because the French said, "Hey, he's a *writer*."

The same thing happened with William Faulkner. He was discovered in France before this country, and the same thing with Philip K. Dick—the greatest science-fiction writer who ever lived, probably. He was just taken seriously in this country in his last few years. He was being invited to France as an honored guest at literary gatherings and so on. In this country, "Oh hell, he's just a science-fiction writer!"

Did you know him?

Only slightly. I only met him a couple of times. However, some dingbat has put into print the idea that Phil Dick went crazy, and not only that, he went crazy from reading my books!

Oh, no! It's a compliment, in a way?

Yeah, I think it's a compliment that I could unhinge a

mind like *his*! I don't think I influenced him that much. He was writing a lot like me before I was writing like me, so to speak. He didn't influence me that much, either, because I developed my style and my technique independently of him, and *then* I discovered he was doing things similar to what I was doing. And when we met we had an immediate empathy. We felt we understood each other very deeply.

He also regarded the universe as a puzzle rather than as a thing known. A labyrinth—that's Joyce's metaphor, too. Somebody could write a good Ph.D dissertation on the metaphor of the labyrinth in James Joyce, Philip K. Dick, and Robert Anton Wilson. We all regard the universe as a maze that we're running around in and trying to figure out.

Turn that recorder off for a minute. Anybody want a drink?

◆ ◆

In Ireland, the pub is a meeting place. In some ways, it's nice because in America you invite somebody to your home and then you get nervous. You run around cleaning everything, and dusting and moving things, and so on. It's much nicer to meet in a pub.

When I was in England, I went to just one pub in Sheffield, and it was like being in a big living room with little booths. It was for the whole family—there wasn't that segregation of age and type.

In Irish pubs, there's always a couple of tables with an old granny sitting there with her straight whiskey. I don't know why, but the old women in Ireland all seem to prefer to drink it straight. Straight whiskey, no water, no ice, you know—gulp! And then they wait about 20 minutes and say "Ahem, ahem!" "You want another?" Down it goes, and then she sits there for another twenty minutes. "Oh, you want another?"

That's one thing that really bothers me about this society—it's almost impossible to get out of this frame of just a few years either way of your own age. You *never* meet people really young, or really old.

Yeah, I know. Somehow my wife and I have transcended that.

Well, *you* would, natch!

We've got friends who are 30 years younger than us. But most people don't. I don't know how we did it, we just broke out of it somehow or other.

No, it's because of your thought. But this is kind of a built-in structure in society that has always really bothered me.

Well, Americans are afraid of one another. I don't know how that happened, exactly. America does have about the highest crime rate in the world. The Irish aren't afraid of one another, so they socialize more easily. Americans don't want to know anybody until they get a proper introduction from somebody who says, "He's okay, he's not going to rape you or rip off your jewels." The Irish don't have that fear of strangers. I don't blame the Americans for being that way, considering what the crime rate is like here. I don't pick up hitchhikers!

In America, they want you to live in perpetual danger.

The Irish police are unarmed.

Yeah! And the British, it's fantastic!

If you disarmed the American police, they'd all be dead in 24 hours! You wouldn't have a police force left. There's something about an Irish policeman that gives you a different feeling than an American policeman, and the fact they're disarmed is part of it. But it's also the whole culture—nobody regards the police as their enemy. Well, nobody except those who are running guns for the IRA. The cops are friendly and people are friendly with the cops. It's an entirely different social *gestalt.*

Is the recorder on or off?

Yeah, I turned it on.

Oh, you turned it back on again. So we're talking about the Irish police.

There are friends of ours who keep the tape recorder on all the time.

When I lived in Berkeley, Tim Leary was trying to persuade me I should have... what the hell do you call it? I'm all for the computer revolution but I don't know much about it. I'm too busy with other things. He wanted me to have my living room networking with a thousand people all around the world. Not because he thought I was that bright, but because of all the interesting people I always had in my living room.

Yeah. The art of conversation...

Actually, Tim does think I'm pretty bright. You can carry modesty too far. He does think I'm pretty bright, so I might as well admit that. That's just his opinion, of course. The editor of the *Bay Guardian* thinks I'm a Satanist.

That's unbelievable!

I want to get that into print, you see! I've mentioned that a couple of times so you don't edit it out. I've heard some weird things on this tour. One television show in L.A. wouldn't have me on because I'm too controversial. That's the first time it's ever been said, honestly. "Me? Controversial?"

Well, I did two interviews yesterday, and I'm quite willing to go on with this for a while, but you've got to ask a question. Don't expect me to give questions as well as the answers! I'm just afraid you'll run out of tape.

Oh no, don't worry. I have a backup.

Well, what else do you want to ask me about? Or should I suggest a topic?

I'm still interested in more elaboration on how you get the interesting information that you've found.

Yeah, you've brought that up a few times.

Well, in the last few years I've been traveling a lot. One of the hazards of these tours is that I always have to get another bag... one more than I started with, because people give me so many books! This tour I got a break when my oldest daughter got a bright idea: "Why don't you leave all these books here and I'll mail them to you in Ireland so you don't have to carry them!" So now, all the books I've collected so far on this tour I don't have to carry from stop to stop—they're going to get mailed to me in Ireland. People give me books, pamphlets, magazines. I acquire a tremendous collection on these tours.

A lot of people give me stuff I don't want. They come up to me after lectures and say, "I've been working ten years on this book and I can't get it published—please read it and tell me how to get it published." As if *I* know how to get published—I'm struggling all the time to get my *own* stuff published... and they think I can just wave a magic wand and get *them* published!

So that's it—a lot of stuff is given to you, so you don't even have to look for it.

I do a lot of looking, too—I'm looking for important stuff all the time. But also, important stuff is looking for me, now! Also, a lot of nonsense is looking for me!

I get all sorts of manuscripts from people who have been contacted by extraterrestrials and whatnot. I got a manuscript sent to me on numerology which I couldn't understand. When I moved, I just threw it out—I didn't want to pack it. A year later, I got a letter from this guy who was very angry that I hadn't responded to him, and he wanted his book back. I thought, "Jesus, he really sent me the *only copy*? Or is this some kind of maneuver to force me to comment on his book?" So I ignored him...

but I felt faintly guilty about it ever since. What are you going to do—you get so many of these things dumped on you and you can't read them *all*. I tried to read that, and I couldn't make any sense out of it.

Do you pay to subscribe to magazines in Ireland?

Well, no. My wife and I had subscriptions to a lot of magazines. They were all due for renewal about the time we decided to move to Ireland. Then we decided not to renew any of them because we weren't sure how long we would stay in Ireland. Then we subscribed to *New Scientist*, and now I've re-subscribed to *Brain/Mind Bulletin* because I miss it so much. That's the best way to keep in touch with developments in psychology and neurology. It's a very good journal.

What are other ones that sound as intriguing as that?

Well, we used to subscribe to a lot, as I said, but we let them all lapse. I used to get *Long Life*, which was a magazine devoted entirely to what was going on in the field of longevity research. Also *Scientific American*, *Science Digest*. A lot of occult publications—I think they're mostly nonsense, but they do have something of value occasionally.

Once in a while, yeah. You might have rejected this one book the author sent you on numerology, but I'll bet you give *some* credence to numerology. I notice numbers occasionally in the news, or even numbers that seem to have personal significance now and then. Certain days seem more favorable than others. Is this superstition, or what?

Well, I do think there's something to the Jungian idea of

synchronicity. I'm not satisfied with Jung's theory—I'm just satisfied that what he's theorizing about is a real phenomenon.

I'm looking for a better theory than Jung's. There *are* meaningful coincidences. We do need a theory to explain them, I think. A lot of them, in my case, have been connected with numbers.

What parts of Jung do you take objection to?

Well, I just feel synchronicity is not a scientific theory. It's a sketch of a theory—not complete enough to be a theory. I think Sheldrake's "morphogenetic field" comes closer to being a scientific theory—testable and demonstrable. Every place I go, people ask me if there's any more research on Sheldrake.

I'm not blaming Jung. It takes a while to get an impression and into the form where it can be expressed in words at all. And then it takes even longer to get it into words that are sharp enough that you can make a scientific test on it.

I also think Bell's theorem is better than synchronicity. Bell's theorem may or may not refer to synchronicity, but it refers to something similar and it *is* testable.

So I'm looking for things better than Jung's writings, although I give him a lot of credit for bringing the subject to attention. And he certainly has had a major influence on the social sciences—it extends way beyond psychology. A lot of social scientists are interested in synchronous phenomena.

Do you find certain numbers more favorable to you, like the number three, for example?

No, I've never noticed anything like that. I've just noticed that coincidences do happen with numbers.

Burroughs makes a lot of the number 23.

Yeah, that's happened a lot in my life. Ever since I met Burroughs I've had the 23 phenomena following me around. I seem to have had a stronger case of it than Burroughs has.

Really?

Well, as far as I know. He hasn't written as much about it as I have. I don't know which of us has noticed more of it. 666, too—that pops up in the damnedest places. One time I was having a manuscript Xeroxed and I had a book about Aleister Crowley in my hand. The guy put down the original, the Xerox and the bill. And I put down the book by Crowley, which had Crowley's picture on the back. I reached for my wallet and looked at the bill. There's Crowley's face and right next to it: $6.66!

That's great!

Well, a thing like that wouldn't impress me too much, except things like that have happened *several times* to me. I've had several 666s pop up in weird conjunctions with Crowley, or with other things I'm investigating that somehow relate to Crowley.

What do you think of Crowley's writing?

There are several aspects to Crowley. First, I like Crowley's methodology, which is to do your *own* experiments in the area of the occult and the mystical. He gives you exercises to do, like these rituals I was talking about earlier, and various yogic exercises. He tells you how to meditate and gives you different forms of meditation: how to do pranayama, and so on.

Together with that, he tells you to be ruthlessly

skeptical about all results, which I think is exactly the right approach. So many people are too damn naïve about any of the phenomena they get out of these experiments. They're altogether too credulous. I like Crowley's approach: be skeptical. The results are mind-blowing enough, no matter how skeptical you are. If you start indulging in extravagant speculations, you can really go off your nut entirely.

Aside from that, there's the question of Crowley's philosophy, which is so hard to categorize. I coined the term anarcho-fascism to describe it broadly, and that's exactly what I think of it. I think it's got attractive features and dangerous features.

Kind of fascist in practice and anarchist in theory, it seems like—

Something like that, yeah. Crowley was a very complicated individual. On the one hand, he had a great sense of humor, and I can't really dislike anybody with a great sense of humor. On the other hand, the sense of humor was pretty cruel and sadistic at times. And then he obviously had his own neurotic compulsions and hang-ups.

Plus a big heroin problem—

Oh yeah—*that,* too! But what I admire about Crowley is that he made damn sure it was impossible for anybody to glorify him or whitewash him. He made sure it all got on record: everything that was wrong with him, so nobody can turn him into a little tin god. I admire that tremendously. He was aware of that danger and he protected himself against it. I mean you've got to learn from Crowley—you can't become a Crowleyan. Nobody can turn Aleister Crowley into a guru figure or a savior, or anything like that. So I admire that about him.

But they *do* and they *have*.

Well, they just haven't read Crowley very carefully. He makes fun of himself all over the place. And one of my favorite texts in *The Book of Lies* is "Frater Perdurabo is nothing but an eye; what eye none knoweth."

Frater Perdurabo is Crowley himself. It took me a long time to decipher that by picking up the clues and jokes elsewhere and the references to his other books. I finally found out the eye is a symbol of the *anus* in Egyptian mythology! He gives you enough clues that you've got to go into Egyptian mythology to understand this book. He's saying, "I'm an asshole and I know it." But most of his disciples are incapable of recognizing jokes like that.

What do you think of magic societies in the world today, as far as what you would deem "worthy activities"?

I suspend judgment.

As to evaluating them, you mean?

Yeah. I think I have more confidence in the Sufis than in most such groups. But that doesn't mean I trust everybody who calls himself a Sufi. As for other magical societies, I think they run the gamut from the absolutely batty to the comparatively sane. I haven't seen any that are really inspiring.

Are there any occult writers who you think are comparatively sane?

Israel Regardie.

He's very active these days.

He's absolutely sane, I think, and absolutely honest. And that's very rare in that field.

Have you met him?

No. We corresponded quite a bit but somehow or other we never met. I wish we had now that he's dead. I wish I had made more effort to have a personal meeting with him.

He just *died*?

He just died a few months ago, yes.

Oh, I didn't know that. I thought you could still go to Arizona and meet him. I've always had that hope.

His last book just came out: *An Interview with Israel Regardie: His Final Thoughts and Views*. It's a long interview with him. I find it a fascinating book because it represents Regardie's views at the end of his life. He says a lot of very perceptive things, and he especially says a lot of the things I've been saying: do the exercises and be skeptical about the results. And don't believe anything too quickly.

He also was terrified that people might turn *him* into a guru of some sort, and he made sure they couldn't. He's joking all through the interview about how drunk he is, just so nobody will take him too seriously! "How many Bloody Marys have I had now?" That sort of thing.

Did you ever read David Conway's book *Magic*?

Yes, that's a pretty good book—that is one of the better books in the field. He's very good about the results of magic being like what the Lady of Shalott saw in the mirror. But so is ordinary perception, as he points out.

We're not given a structure in our society to research this topic. An awful lot of it seems very adolescent—

—very adolescent and very simplistic... and often *hysterical.* I think we're still, to some extent, suffering from the after-effects of the Holy Inquisition in which all forms of mysticism or consciousness-altering technologies were condemned by the church as satanic and heretical, and so on. And so what survived did so underground, and usually with a habit of secrecy and concealment that hasn't quite been outgrown yet. Most occult orders have their inner secrets. If you join a few of them you find out the secrets are the same in all of them, and they're all busy hiding the same stuff.

It works best when it's open and honest—

Exactly. I think the main problem with Western occultism is its tradition of secrecy. I've done my best to smash that by publishing all the occult secrets I know, as far and wide as I can!

Are there any secrets anymore? It seems that a lot of the prized manuscripts have in recent years been reprinted.

Well, it's like the secrets of Freemasonry. The secrets of Freemasonry are so carefully hidden that no non-Mason can find them out without spending at least two or three days in rare bookstores. [laughter] It's the same with occult secrets. You can find them out if you're curious enough.

I know all the secrets of Masonry, I think. That's a rather extravagant claim, I know. Just by browsing around in rare bookstores looking for old books, and so on. And I've tested this by talking to Masons. Some of them have broken the conversations off abruptly when they realized

what they were getting into and that I wasn't a Mason.
But I've run into some who don't believe in the secrecy
and are willing to have friendly joking conversations, in
which I test whether these alleged books that reveal the
secrets of Masonry are accurate. They're accurate *enough*.
Masons know what I'm talking about when I talk about
the Widow's Son, or the secret of the 9th Degree, and so
on.

So you can find the secrets out if you're curious
enough. You can find the secrets of Masonry and occultism
and alchemy if you want to. And everything has been

published recently anyway. **Culling's *A Manual of Sex Magic* will tell you everything about the inner secrets of the OTO, and most of what you might want to know about alchemy to boot.**

I've pretty much published all of this in one place or another. There are some secrets of Masonry I won't reveal, though, just out of a sense of courtesy (or something). Some of the rituals are most effective if the candidate doesn't know what's going to happen next, so I don't want to spoil the surprise ending by giving it away.

When I write about Masonic rituals, I generally change them a little, just so people who have read me—if they're going to go through the Masonic initiations—will be surprised anyway. The Masonic ritual in *The Earth Will Shake* is partly based on the real Masonic initiation, and partly it's based on initiations of two other occult orders that I was initiated in at one time or another. So anybody who gets initiated as a 1st Degree Mason thinking they are going to go through what I described in that book is going to get a hell of a shock. They are going to find something *else* happening entirely. Only part of what I describe is the actual 1st Degree ritual. I don't want to be more explicit than that. As I said, I don't want to spoil the surprise for anybody.

I thought the Masons had become more of a social business club, like the Elks.

It depends on how high you go. Masons, as a general rule (it is my impression), are not encouraged to go for the higher degrees. But if anybody shows *promise,* they are encouraged to go for the higher degrees. And then they find out there's more to Masonry than most Masons realize. That's part of the reason for the degree system.

Some of the paranoid things written against Masons are almost true. Except that it's a matter of where you are looking from. What I mean about them being almost true is that the paranoids claim the Masons are out to destroy Christianity, for instance. Well, they're *not* out to destroy Christianity, but Masonry really *is* an attempt to destroy intolerance. It's an attempt to educate and enlighten people to the stage where all forms of bigotry and intolerance are *transcended*. And so from the point of view of fundamentalists, that is an attack on Christianity. But from a point of view of any rational person, it's just an attempt to spread enlightenment and common humanity, you know?

People might have trouble reconciling that with the idea that upper-level Masons are involved in government—

I keep saying you shouldn't have *one* model. Here I give you a Marxist model. This I have pondered a great deal: Why was Masonry so revolutionary in the 18th century? Why is it connected to very conservative groups, generally, in the 20th century? I think the best model for that is the Marxist model. In the 18th century, Masonry was the ideology of the revolutionary class, which was the bourgeoisie. Now the bourgeoisie is the entrenched class, and so Masonry is the ideology of entrenched class, so it's become more conservative. And I think that explains why Robespierre was a—*was* Robespierre a Mason? Well anyway, Danton was, and Marat was, and Jefferson was. Most of the French and American revolutionaries were Freemasons, and in the 20th century, you find Harry Truman and J. Edgar Hoover are Masons. J. Edgar Hoover is enough to let you know Masonry is not as revolutionary as it once was.

And was he an upper initiate?

J. Edgar Hoover was a 33rd Degree.

Good grief.

So was FDR. Adlai Stevenson was a Freemason. Gerald Ford—he was 33rd Degree.

Gerald Ford?!

Yeah. I've been told Ronald Reagan is a Freemason, but I'm not sure. My source for that was just a letter from somebody who claimed to know. I don't know if it's been verified. But I would expect it—most of the presidents have been Freemasons. It's very hard to find a president who clearly was *not* a Freemason. Most of them have been. The others that you're not sure of, they probably were considering their connections—they were connected with a lot of Freemasons, usually in politics. The general strategy seems to be: any Freemason that gets nominated for president is elevated to the 33rd Degree right away, making them go through all the stages in between.

I would have thought it'd be a learning process.

They sort of accelerate it if you get nominated for president.

Speed learning. Like an honorary degree from a university—

That's right, it's very much like an honorary degree.

Have you read R.A. Schwaller de Lubicz? He's an Egyptologist.

No. I read Budge's translation of the *Book of the Dead* and I found out where the Grateful Dead got their name.

Yeah, exactly! You'd probably like R.A. Schwaller

de Lubicz. He's seemingly quite rational. He unfolds sort of a whole symbol system based just on natural symbols that you can recognize. He just interprets them. That's one of the values—his interpretation of the whole of nature as a huge assemblage of symbols. They have occult meanings, they embody principles.

What's his name again?

Schwaller de Lubicz. He was also an alchemist. He replicated stained glass, like at Notre Dame. He kept a very low-key life.

◆ ◆

Well, we're always, of course, concerned with how we can more or less "evolve" or enlarge our vision. We're always asking people to help us in that direction—

How to evolve? Read my book *Prometheus Rising* and do all the exercises in that. There are lots of exercises; it will keep you busy for at least a year. And if at the end of the year you haven't evolved, write me a letter of complaint and I'll try to write a better book. [laughing]

What are your current obsessions?

Well, I'm still working on the *Illuminatus* novels. My current research is on the French and American revolutions. I'm doing more research on that than I've done in the past. I'm looking for more information on various aspects of the great upheaval of the 18th century.

What else am I researching these days? I'm always looking for more data on what's happening in quantum mechanics and non-local connection. What new arguments have been brought up against it by those who don't like the non-local connection? And I'm always interested in anything new about Sheldrake.

I have a two-hour lecture to do tonight.

How would you feel about us taping the lecture tonight?

Oh, that's fine with me. Yes, print the lecture along with the interview. Yes, that would be fine with me.

When you moved from Berkeley to Ireland, did you leave anything behind, like an archive or a library?

Arlen and I donated most of our books. Shipping books is expensive. So we only shipped the ones we were most attached to, and we donated all the rest to Hawthorn University.

What does your wife do? Does she write, too?

She writes poetry, and she writes an occasional article, usually under a pen name. We have different approaches to writing. She doesn't like publicity. She prefers to write under pen names rather than attract a lot of attention. Her sister was an actress and quit acting. Arlen just has this general feeling that becoming a celebrity is a major calamity. And sometimes I think she's right. [laughs]

Well, we won't print anything that we think could make you look bad. That's our goal.

No, no I'm not worried about that. I'm used to criticism. I'm hardly a celebrity yet. Herb Caen called me a "mini-celebrity" once. That may be accurate.

That's better, because then you can walk down the

street and travel without getting harassed. You've got a lot of mobility still—that's good.

Yeah, but I'm losing it more all the time. I'm beginning to see why a lot of people couldn't deal with being a celebrity, like Freddie Prinze, Sr.

Oh no, don't do that. Murder, not suicide.

No, I don't mean I'm in any danger of that, but I see the tensions involved. People who admire an artist seem to feel they *own* part of the artist. They can be astonishingly insensitive and intrusive. I can understand why people like Danny Kaye got a reputation for being notoriously hostile to fans. Fans can really try to devour you! And they feel very righteous about it, too: I *admire* you, therefore I *own* you. Therefore *stand still and let me eat you!*

Really, it can be quite disconcerting at times. My last year in San Francisco before I moved to Ireland—people would show up at my door when I was trying to write. If I try to get rid of them in like 10 minutes, they'd be quite offended. They wanted three hours of my time because they are fans of mine, and what kind of snot am I that I wouldn't be friendly to my fans? But if I let three of them in, in a day, that's 30 hours and the day only has 24 hours. I have no time to sleep, much less write.

You've got to push them out, you know. It's amazing how people can be. Their own egos are so damn important, they don't realize that I've got a life of my own to lead. That's another reason I like living in a little fishing village nine miles from Dublin: it's harder for them to find me. As a matter of fact, don't mention the name of the village I live in. That's giving them too many clues. [laughter]

No, we won't give out your address.

And phone calls, *migod!* I finally got an unlisted phone

before we left here because we'd get them all day. Some of these nuts would call in the middle of the night! You get people calling at 3 in the morning. Just because you're a writer and they like you, they think they have a right to any amount of your time that they want to seize. Nobody can realize what it's like until it starts happening. After a lecture, I want to go with a few friends and have a drink to relax. Oh jesus, trying to escape! I've been studying Tim Leary—he's worked out the escape technique, and he's got it down to a science.

Really?

You see Tim at a lecture. He disappears in a puff of smoke. He knows just how to escape before they can all descend on him.

That's funny! I was going to ask you one thing but I don't know if you'll grant it. When we interviewed J.G. Ballard, we printed a book list of part of his library. Can you give me a list of some books from your library?

Well, okay. How long do you want it to be? Twenty books, or fifty books?

More like 50.

Okay, I'll send you a list of fifty books I currently own. I'm not going to inventory my whole damn library, but I will send you a list of fifty books.

You're going to have an interview *with* me—but how would you like an interview *by* me?

Really? Yeah!

I've got an interview I did with Sean McBride. I sold it to a

Swiss newspaper. I haven't been able to sell it anywhere in the United States. I think it should be printed somewhere in the United States.

Can you send it to us?

Yeah. Do you know who Sean McBride is?

I really don't.

He won the Nobel Peace Prize a few years ago. He's won the American Medal of Justice, the Lenin Peace Prize, the Dag Hammarskjöld Medal of Honor from the United Nations. He's the head of the National Lawyers Guild for Peace. He founded Amnesty International. He's done more than any living human being to get political prisoners released all over the world. And this interview is somewhat dated, and I'll mark the places that are dated—you can change it. Where I say "Reagan's upcoming visit to Ireland", just change it to "Reagan's recent visit to Ireland", and so on. But he said some fascinating things in this interview. He says the United States government is currently guilty of war crimes under the Nuremberg laws.

Of course it is.

Yeah, wait until you read his argument—he's a lawyer. I mean, he's very specific. He says the whole nuclear arms race is a crime under the Nuremberg precedents. Rudolf Hess was convicted of war crimes, even though he didn't commit any.

Right. He was on a peace mission.

He was convicted of *conspiring* to commit war crimes. And so McBride argues that anybody who is involved in a nuclear missile business is conspiring to commit a war crime. I think that should be printed in the United States.

Yeah! Sure, *we'll* print it.

He says a lot of other interesting things, too, about the history of the IRA and the infiltration of the IRA by British intelligence. He speaks out on a lot of subjects. The death squads in Central America and the direct support they're getting from the Reagan administration. This interview was turned down by *Penthouse*, by *Playboy*, by *New Age Magazine*.

New Age?! You're an editor there, how can they turn it down?

That's right. Oh, they turned it down anyway!

They're afraid to print it, then.

You should have seen the letter they sent me about why they wouldn't print it. This letter would seem to me to be a solid 100% hypocrisy.

Send us the letter too—we'll print that!

I much prefer the guy in San Diego who said we can't do anything to offend the Catholic Church. This was such hypocrisy!

As I say, I got paid for this once already—I sold it to a Swiss newspaper, but really I'd like to get it into an American publication. So you can have Wilson as a subject of interview and Wilson as the interviewer of McBride.

That would be great!

I'll send it to you as soon as I get back to Ireland. You

know, I tell you what—I'll do a little editing where it's out of date before I send it to you. I really would love to see that in print in the United States, especially in the Bay Area so the *Bay Guardian* can gnash their teeth that they didn't get it. I'm still pissed off this guy said I'm a Satanist, I don't know what to make of that.

Maybe they're an example of why the left isn't always much better than the right—

Since you do themed issues, let me just show you a little of something else. I never wrote the answers to this because things came up. This is my International Conspiracy Trivia Quiz. Just take a look at a few pages and if you like it, I'll take it back to Ireland with me and I'll write an answer page to go with it. I'll send it back along with the Sean McBride interview, okay?

Yeah! Wow!

Read the first three pages and the last three pages. That'll give you an idea of what it's like. See if you'd like to print this together with the correct answers to the questions.

[laughter as Vale reads the document] Brian De Palma, perfect choice of director! This is great. This is the way this subject should be approached! It should be *fun*! Yes, write the answers! This is perfect.

I happen to like *120 Days of Sodom*—it's such an amazing book.

The correct answer is *The Godfather*. [laughter]

Yeah, I'm sure. I'd like to send you our version of the interview so we can get the spelling all correct. You know, I believe in that.

Yes, I do too. I had an interview done once by an English magazine that didn't check back with me. They misspelled everybody's name they could possibly guess wrong on.

Is this your only copy of this?

Yes.

Do you think we can take it right now to a nearby xerox place?

Yeah, but you still need the answers.

Oh, I know, but I get real nervous when I see this is an only copy of something. We'll find a place and come back with it—

Okay, do that. I'll have another drink while you're out doing that. And then I would like the afternoon off. I've got a lecture this evening and I'd like to lie down and rest for a while.

Of course, lie down, please. Relax the front brain. Well, this is great. I'm really pleased.

Okay, take this and Xerox it, and then from Ireland, I'll send you my Sean McBride interview and the answers. You can have a lot of fun trying to guess.

I think it's going to be great! I already want the answers.

I'll give you one answer. Which one are you most curious about?

One that I think I know the answer. Burroughs said "No government can exist without... bullshit?"

That's right. That's the correct answer to that one, yes.

Burroughs is one of my favorite people. Did you ever meet him?

Oh yes. Is the recorder still on? We might as well include this in the interview. I have the highest possible opinion of Burroughs as a human being and as a writer. I was on a panel discussion in New York about Burroughs's books a few years ago. Brion Gysin was saying that Burroughs is the greatest living American writer and it's a shame that he's recognized as such in Europe but not in America. I said, "Amen, I couldn't agree more."

Burroughs writes so much about homosexuality that people who aren't gay often think his books are just books for gay people. But that's as wrong as saying Raymond Chandler is only a writer for policemen to read because he writes about crime, or Joyce is only for Irish readers.

I think Burroughs is so goddamn great. He writes better than anybody alive. Sentence by sentence, he's the greatest stylist. I think his insight into the pathologies of power—he's beyond Kafka, he sees deeper than Kafka ever saw. He sees deeper than Marx or Machiavelli or Freud or Reich.

I've learned a hell of a lot from Burroughs. **I think the best things in my books probably are inspired by Burroughs.** I think about what Burroughs wrote and then I try to go one step further. And I may go one step back; I don't know. Like Jung said once *apropos* of Freud—people thought Jung was very hostile to Freud after their split, but Jung said, "If I ever see further than Freud, it's because I'm standing on his shoulders." I feel very much I'm standing on Burroughs's shoulders. I don't know why when I mentioned my favorite books I mentioned Tucker and *Science and Sanity* and Nietzsche and I didn't mention Burroughs. Burroughs's novels have had a tremendous influence on me, and I think he's a delightful man. In spite of the horrors he writes about, he's really a very gentle and kind person.

He writes about horror so much because the world horrifies him so much. That's why he was a junkie for so long. By the way, has he relapsed? Is he a junkie again?

No.

I saw a television interview with him and I couldn't tell whether he was joking or not—he was joking about going to the methadone clinic and so on.

Off the record: yeah.

What? He *has* relapsed?

Well, methadone. It's because he had this skin cancer and it was getting painful. He's in his 70s.

Well, I don't judge him by that. Crowley relapsed in his 70s because of his asthma. He decided he'd be happier on heroin than without heroin. I think nobody can judge that except somebody with asthma, you know.

If I were told I had only a couple of months to live, I would buy all the LSD and cocaine I could. I told you I don't think much of cocaine as a long-range thing, but as a short-range thing, I would be doing coke all day to write as much as I could, and doing acid to keep high while waiting for death, you know. I think everybody has the right to decide for themselves, when you're confronting things like death and so on. My choice would be acid and cocaine to prepare for death.

Crowley preferred heroin and he had asthma. I've never had asthma—I might prefer heroin if I had asthma. If Burroughs wants to go back on methadone, that's *his* business.

Did you ever try that ecstasy drug?

Yeah.

What did you think? Because someone just gave me some. I didn't try it.

I suspect that the psychiatrists who think it's very effective as therapy are right. I don't think it's much of a recreational drug. I think that this is even stupider than what happened with LSD. People are going to be buying it *because* the government made it illegal, and it's not much of a recreational drug.

What did you get from it? Do you think I should take it?

What you get from it is: you feel good. You feel good all over. It's a body drug to some extent, like grass. It makes you tingle and relax and feel happy with your body. But in conversation, you find you're listening more closely to other people and there's less competition and more sharing. And I'm convinced that psychiatrists who say that they've had marvelous results... I'm convinced that's because the patient is able to *relax* enough.

The main problem in therapy is telling the patient to take charge of his own life and the patient feels he can't. I think ecstasy works so well in therapy because the psychiatrist says, "Well, why don't you do *so-and-so?*" and the patient doesn't come up with a lot of rationalizations, saying "I can't." He suddenly hears it and thinks "Well, why *don't* I?!"

Like people with unhappy marriages—usually, the best answer is to end the marriage. You know, some people go on for years and years. If the therapist says, "Well, why don't you just end the marriage?" "Well, I can't do that because I'd feel guilty and because this would happen and that would happen." And on ecstasy, "Yeah, why *don't* I end the marriage?"

One therapist I was speaking to told me that he's got a lot of people off cocaine with just one session with ecstasy. All he does is at the right point say, "Well, if it's giving you that much trouble, why don't you just quit?" And the guy says, "Yeah, of course I can quit!" And stops rationalizing: "Well, it's such an addiction, I can't control it..." And they *do* quit. I think it's probably very powerful in therapy.

People are going to be trying ecstasy for thrills because the government made it illegal, and they are going to be disappointed. And also they are going to be getting a lot of crap, like happened in '68: there was so damn much PCP around San Francisco being sold as acid. The PCP may come out of the closets and be sold as ecstasy now. God forbid. I feel sorry for the people who are buying it.

◆ ◆

There's so much poverty in Ireland that nobody feels humiliated, degraded or dehumanized by being poor. They just accept it. They make jokes about it. And everybody knows their grandparents were poor. If they're lucky, they know it's just a recent thing. There's been so much poverty in Ireland that it's not disgraceful. Like when I went to the Boyne Valley, an American tourist asked the tour guide, "What do you do in the winter when you're not leading these tours?" He said, "I'm a government artist." She said, "A government artist?" He said, "Yeah, I draw the dole."

The Irish are always joking... There's a lot of partial unemployment there as well as full unemployment, and they will joke about it. Nobody's ashamed of it. They do have a lot of poverty. And the Catholic Church has too much control over politics there. But I'm very happy that there's so much resistance to it. There never was in Irish history before. The intellectuals traditionally went into exile—they decided that they couldn't fight the church, so they ran away—they wrote their books in London or Paris. Now they're staying in Ireland and fighting the church, and I think they're going to win. Attacking the church is the major occupation of the Irish intelligentsia, and I'm all for it.

Your daughters, what do they do? Do they live here?

One of them lives on the California coast, the other lives in Silicon Valley. My son lives on the coast, too. My oldest daughter is living with a computer programmer and back in college studying biology. She wants to make nature films, so she's studying films and majoring in biology. The other daughter runs a telephone answering service and is on the loans committee of the credit union. They picked her as the most promising businesswoman of the year, according to their loans committee. And my son is in college, still. He's the youngest of the three. The one who runs the answering service, she has more credit than I have. That amazes me: she's so successful in business. I never thought she'd turn out that way, but of course, that's not the whole story on her. She's also got a black belt in karate. And she spent over a year on an ashram in India. So being a businesswoman is only one aspect of this young lady's life.

Where have you traveled over the world?

I haven't traveled nearly as much...

Have you ever been to India?

No, I've never been to the Orient at all. I keep looking forward to that. So far I don't have enough fans in the Orient or anybody to invite me to lecture there. No,

I've been around Europe and the United States. I got to Hawaii once. I've been in Canada a few times. I'm going back to Canada next week. But I haven't seen any part of Africa or Asia yet. I'm really looking forward to that. I'm waiting for the opportunity. If nobody invites me to give a lecture, I hope a magazine will send me there to do a story. I want to see Japan, I want to see China.

All my life I've been reading propaganda about China, pro and con. The American line on China and the Maoist line. I'd like to see China for myself. What the hell is really happening there? I don't believe anybody's propaganda. I'd like to see for myself. And I want to see and be a... I'm not that mad about Tibet, for some reason. Who wants to go to Tibet? If that's possible I'll do it, but don't have a mad rush to get to Tibet. For that matter, I'd like to see Australia just for the hell of it. The Australians have such a notorious reputation. I want to see if they're as bad as their reputation. They have the kind of reputation that the Irish used to have.

You might find yourself in Tahiti and settle down there like Brando did for a while.

Oh yeah.

Are you going to be coming back here in the next year?

I'll be back here in March. I don't know if I'll be in San Francisco, but I'm going to be in California in March.

Let us know where you're going to be. Maybe we'll come to see you or hear you.

Well, I'm doing four lectures in the L.A. area and I'm doing a seminar at the Ojai Institute. I don't know what else I'll be doing in California. Those are the bookings that are solid; the others are up in the air. I may be doing a lecture in Palo Alto—that hasn't been finalized yet. But anyway, I'll be in the state for at least a couple of weeks. I'm also supposed to appear in Eugene, Oregon and somewhere in Alaska. I don't know if I want to go to Alaska in March. I think I'd rather go to Alaska in July. I don't know what Alaska is like in March. Well, it'll be the end of March, April.

Can we take a photo?

Yeah, sure. I'm so bloody tired. It'll be easy because I won't try to look attractive, I'll just try to look awake. You know, I've been interviewed by two Punk magazines. One here in the Bay Area a couple of years ago. And *Hot Press* in Dublin. They interviewed me recently. That's in this month's issue. I haven't seen it yet but my wife wrote me a letter saying it was a great interview, but I look shaggy in the photo. The photographer insisted on taking me down to the waterfront to get dramatic backgrounds of the islands off the coast of Howth, with the ocean and the islands and waves splashing. In that kind of wind, of course, my hair is blowing all over the place!

That's what the photographer wanted. I think he thought it would make me look macho or something. But my wife just thought I looked shaggy. Why do they take photographs of people with their hair blowing in the wind? They do it with women too. What do they do that? Photographers love that effect. And all that happens is whoever you're living with says you look unkempt.

You can just imagine one of those big movie fans positioned off-screen somewhere.

That's like *Three Godfathers*, that John Ford movie with the windstorm in it? There was no windstorm in the script, and the windstorm came up. John Ford said, "This

is too good to miss!" So he improvised a scene with all the actors out in the windstorm. And the critic in the *New Yorker* described the scene as, "The most convincing windstorm the wind machines of Hollywood have ever produced."

You know this picture of Truman Capote on the couch lying down? I don't think we want to imitate that.

Well, we had Ballard lying down... Yes, like you're in deep rapture thinking of the next book.

Let's do a Bogart.

Oh yeah. Okay. That's like Hemingway!

I met Hemingway once.

You did?

I was very young then. So you know what I said? I said, "Gee, I really like your books, sir." I wish I had all that to do over again—I'd say something more intelligent. [laughter] I was a clerk in a bookstore and Hemingway came in. And I said, "Gee, I really like your books, sir." And so after he was through browsing around, he bought the books to me to be checked out. He bought three books on bullfighting by writers I'd never heard of (who were nowhere near as good as he was), and a book about a boy and his dog. That's my one Hemingway story.

What city was that in?

New York, the Doubleday bookstore on 52nd & 5th. That's the biggest store they have in New York, I think.

I think it closed down.
Oh, it did? Well, that was a long time ago—well over 30

years ago.

We'll send our William Burroughs book.

Oh yes, I'd love to see that.

It has Burroughs and Brion Gysin.

So I'm going to send you one chapter from the *The New Inquisition*, the answers to the quiz, and also my Sean McBride interview.

And the book list!

You're going to like the Sean McBride interview. Even if *Playboy* and *Penthouse* didn't like it, *you're* going to like it. This is a great old man. He's 84 or 85. He's even more optimistic than I am, despite all the horrors he's seen.

He's an Irishman?

Oh yeah, he's very Irish. You can't get much more Irish. His father was shot by the British in 1916. His mother was Maud Gonne. You ever heard of her? Yeats wrote a lot of poems about her. When Sean McBride was a little boy she introduced him to Ho Chi Minh at an anti-imperialist congress in Frankfurt. Isn't it funny how things connect up? I think he met Lenin at the same congress. Sean McBride has seen a lot of history and participated in a lot of it.

And god, I'm tired! I've got to lay down.

Yeah. Please do. Okay, bye.

◆ ◆ ◆

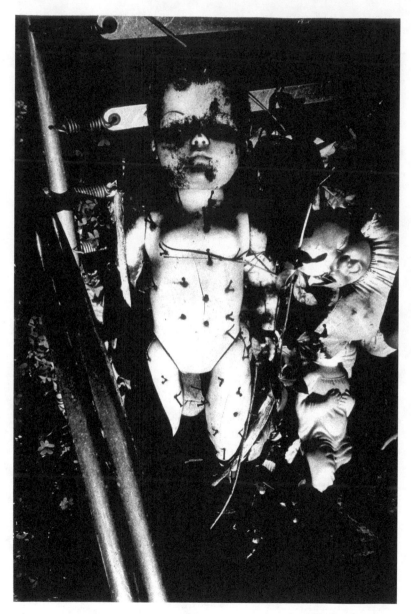

Photo: Yoshi Yubai

Letters from
ROBERT ANTON WILSON

In these letters Wilson submits material to RE/Search for a proposed special issue. They offer a glimpse into the collaborative process, and Wilson's thoughts at the time.

1. Letter from Wilson (24 September 1985)

> 3 The Haggard
> Howth,
> Dublin
> Ireland
> 24 September 1985

Dear Vale,

Enclosed are the items I promised to send you, along with a few others I thought you might want to use.

Up front is the list of about 50 books from my library, which proved less boring to me than I expected, and convinced me you were right in asking for it, since I guess others will find it, as I did, an amusing montage. Following is a poem which I recently committed (on return to Ireland) and which you might like. Then, inspired by the Ballard issue, I add two collages of a sort. Then comes the international conspiracy trivia quiz, with answers, and slightly rewritten—local Irish jokes replaced by American

jokes. Next, chapter one from *The New Inquisition*, which seems to be the only chapter suitable for publication out of context. Then the Sean MacBride interview, with a note on the curious fact that it was easier to sell in Europe than the US. Finally, a piece on Jung and physics previously published only in Germany.

Please drop me a quick line to reassure me that you received all this safely.

It was a great pleasure meeting you, and I look forward to receiving and correcting the interview. I was pretty exhausted that day and I'm sure the style and even the grammar need a lot of improvement.

In the MacBride interview I have boxes around sentences which, I suggest, could be listed out and used as sub-heads on pages. This is because I think MacBride is not as well-known in America as in Europe and I want something to draw the reader into that piece. You as editors are, of course, at liberty to reject this suggestion.

Do you know how many Punks it takes to change a light-bulb? Two—one to change the bulb and one to kick the chair out from under him.

Live long and prosper,
Robert Anton Wilson

> The reality of metaphysics is the reality of masks.
> Oscar Wilde

> How can you tell the dancer from the dance?
> W.B. Yeats

> Don't just eat a hamburger—eat the HELL out of it.
> J.R. "Bob" Dobbs

2. Letter from Wilson (9 December 1985)

3 The Haggard
Howth
Dublin, Ireland
9 December 1985

Dear Vale,

Thanks for your kind letter of 4 November.

Don't have much to say except that... hmmm. I've been in Basel to do a seminar, Zurich to visit Joyce's grave while in Switzerland, Frankfurt to do interviews with German mags during the Book Fair (at expense of my German publisher) and in Amsterdam to do a lecture and seminar... Looked into the Rembrandt museum & the Van Gogh museum while in Amsterdam; Rembrandt inspires profound respect but Vincent inspires AWE.

You might add this to your RAW issue:

SELF-REFERENTIAL SURREALIST HAIKU

READING NEWSPAPER HEADLINES CAUSES
BRAIN TO SHRINK
LEADING SCIENTISTS SAY:
HAIKU ALSO "POSSIBLY HAZARDOUS"

I wrote that for a friend in New York who was hoping to persuade Goodyear to project 100 new haiku on their blimp one Sunday afternoon over Manhattan. From what I hear, Goodyear is not cordial to the idea... so it goes.

Of course, it's not a pure haiku—no seasonal reference etc. Well, it's ONLY a surrealist haiku, then.

I suggested to said friend that he get permission from Burroughs to use the following also-surrealist haiku (from THE THIRD MIND):

> God-damned floating whorehouse
> Death is the navigator

But the reply was "My God, Goodyear will never go for that." So it goes.

At a gallop, mud-splattered, high in oath,
Robert Anton Wilson

[Enclosed with the letter was a magazine advertisement for an "authentic miracle crucifix", delivered with a certificate of authenticity attesting to the fact that it contains "1) water actually drawn from the Spring of Miracles in Lourdes, France, 2) Earth actually gathered from the Holy Site in Bethlehem where Jesus was born, 3) a genuine-faceted .25 pt precious Diamond, 4) a genuine blood-red previous Ruby jewel, and 5) genuine layered Gold Dorée of 24 Karats content."]

50 books from the library of ROBERT ANTON WILSON

— *The Complete Books of Charles Fort*, Charles Fort
— *The Book as World: James Joyce's Ulysses*, Marilyn French
— *Cities of the Red Night*, William S. Burroughs
— *Physics as Metaphor*, Roger S. Jones
— *A Second Census of Finnegans Wake*, Adaline Glasheen
— *Joyce's Politics*, Dominic Manganiello
— *The I Ching and the Genetic Code: The Hidden Key to Life*, Martin Schönberger
— *The Cantos*, Ezra Pound
— *A Gaelic Lexicon for Finnegans Wake*, Brendan O'Hehir
— *The Lazy Man's Guide to Death and Dying*, E.J. Gold
— *The Age of Napoleon*, Will & Ariel Durant
— *The Permanent War Economy: American Capitalism in Decline*, Seymour Melman
— *The Best of Myles*, Myles na Gopaleen (Flann O'Brien)
— *The New Existentialism*, Colin Wilson
— *Jack the Ripper: The Final Solution*, Stephen Knight
— *ABC of Reading*, Ezra Pound
— *The Rainbow Cadenza*, J. Neil Schulman
— *Station Island*, Seamus Heaney
— *The Four-Gated City*, Doris Lessing
— *The Rat on Fire*, George V. Higgins
— *Liber Aleph*, Aleister Crowley
— *Archetypes: A Natural History of the Self*, Anthony Stevens
— *Critical Path*, R. Buckminster Fuller
— *Farewell, My Lovely*, Raymond Chandler
— *Revisionist Viewpoints: Essays in a Dissident Historical Tradition*, James J. Martin
— *Beethoven*, Maynard Solomon

- *Red Harvest*, Dashiell Hammett
- *Personae*, Ezra Pound
- *Passage of Arms*, Eric Ambler
- *In God's Name: An Investigation into the Murder of Pope John Paul I*, David Yallop
- *The Vatican Connection*, Richard Hammer
- *Hermes to His Son Thoth, Being Joyce's Use of Giordano Bruno in Finnegans Wake*, Frances M. Boldereff
- *Yeats*, Frank Tuohy
- *Joysprick: An Introduction to the Language of James Joyce*, Anthony Burgess
- *Sean: An Intimate Memoir of Sean O'Casey*, Eileen O'Casey
- *Sabbatical: A Romance*, John Barth
- *Endless Enemies: The Making of an Unfriendly World*, Jonathan Kwitny
- *The Portable Nietzsche*, ed. by Walter Kaufmann
- *Complete Works*, Oscar Wilde
- *Paterson*, William Carlos Williams
- *In Banks We Trust*, Penny Lernoux
- *Living Time and the Integration of Life*, Maurice Nicoll
- *Closing Time*, Norman O. Brown
- *Tales of the Dervishes*, Idries Shah
- *The Pound Era*, Hugh Kenner
- *A Colder Eye: The Modern Irish Writers*, Hugh Kenner
- *Lion of Ireland*, Morgan Llywelyn
- *The Boyne Valley Vision*, Martin Brennan
- *The Book of Lies*, Aleister Crowley
- *Tudor and Stuart Ireland*, Margaret MacCurtain
- *Mastery Through Accomplishment*, Hazrat Inayat Khan
- *The Right Stuff*, Tom Wolfe
- *The Tale of the Tribe: Ezra Pound and the Modern Verse Epic*, Michael André Bernstein
- *The Atrocity Exhibition*, J.G. Ballard

◆ ◆ ◆

Photo opposite: Yoshi Yubai

Lectures offered by
ROBERT ANTON WILSON

Wilson distributed this menu of lectures that he was prepared to present during his tours circa 1985. The list was to be included in the proposed RE/Search special issue on Wilson to promote his availability as a speaker.

Whatever You Say You Are, You Aren't: A New Look at Science and Mysticism

Unlike other approaches to the problem of science's relation to mysticism, this presentation stresses how both disciplines use language in special ways. Wilson also discusses how traditional linguistic habits (in politics, religion, philosophy etc.) literally function as brainwashing devices.

The Universe Contains a Maybe: A Journey Beyond Either/Or

A popular introduction to non-Aristotelian logics, this presentation will discuss von Neumann's Quantum Logic, de Bono's yes-no-po technique for problem solving, Korzybski's General Semantics and the operational logic of Rapoport. The aim is to show that many problems do not exist in the world at all, but are created by our habit of either/or thinking.

Holy Blood, Holy Murder and Counterfeit Stocks: The Decline and Fall of the Roman Catholic Church

Based on Wilson's research for his next novel, this talk

Photo opposite: Yoshi Yubai

presents astonishing facts behind the P2 scandal in Italy and its links with bank frauds, the CIA, the drug industry and the Vatican Bank.

Coincidance: Isomorphism and Synchronicity in *Finnegans Wake* and *I Ching*

Using two of the most remarkable books ever written, this presentation shows that the Jungian collective unconscious has a structure that can be described mathematically and relates directly to the latest discoveries in quantum physics.

The Jumping Jesus Phenomenon: A Basic Introduction to Futurism

A presentation that explains precisely and exactly why there will be more changes in the next 40 years than in the previous 40,000 years, and what you can do about it.

How to Tell Your Friends From the Apes: Primate and Post-Primate Psychology

This presentation shows to what extent humans act like programmed machines (or like conditioned animals in a Behaviorist's lab) and what known techniques exist to conquer our mechanical thoughts-feelings-behaviors to achieve inner freedom and greater creativity.

The New Inquisition: A Skeptical Look at Skepticism

An examination of the techniques used to suppress dissident and unorthodox scientific theories today, as compared to the techniques of the Inquisition. Wilson asks: Has Fundamentalist Materialism become as dogmatic and intolerant as old-style Fundamentalist Religion ever was?

The I in the Triangle: A Seminar by Robert Anton Wilson and Arlen Wilson

This seminar confronts the great anxiety about the future that increasingly dominates and paralyzes our society. Using ideas and exercises from a variety of disciplines, Bob, a psychologist, and Arlen, a sociologist, will demonstrate the extent to which we are all capable of greater creativity and responsibility than we normally realize. The goal: to take responsibility for the future by becoming the only real "Power Elite" in the modern world: the men and women who are not afraid of change and are eager to build a better world.

◆ ◆ ◆

Photo: Yoshi Yubai

International Conspiracy Trivia Quiz

On 18 June 1982 Roberto Calvi, president of the unruly Banco Ambrosiano and prominent member of the Freemasonic "P2" conspiracy, was found hanged from Blackfriars Bridge in London, his pockets full of bricks. The scandals and hullabaloo connected with Calvi and P2 continue to make headlines (and best-selling books) and nearly everybody— from the Pope to Scotland Yard, and from the KGB to the CIA—has come under suspicion in one way or another. Since, after three years, Calvi's death is still unexplained, we present our readers with a new form of trivia game— International Conspiracy trivia. To keep it properly murky, more than one answer to each question may be correct.

1. We all know what happened to Calvi. What happened to his secretary, Graziella Corrocher?
    a. She is now a nun in a convent in Milan
    b. She found work dubbing the voice of Bugs Bunny in Italian versions of the cartoons
    c. She is playing herself in a Brian de Palma movie about Calvi
    d. She jumped or was pushed out of a window of Banco Ambrosiano in Milan the same day Calvi died in London

2. Giuseppe Dellacha was another important executive of Banco Ambrosiano. What happened to him?
    a. He is now under indictment for stock fraud in Italy
    b. He was revealed as a CIA "deep cover" agent and disappeared
    c. He is now a Punk Rock star in Liverpool

d. He jumped or was pushed out of a window of Banco Ambrosiano in Milan in October 1982

3. Calvi said the following was his favorite novel, because it shows the world as it really is:
   a. *War and Peace*, Tolstoy
   b. *The Wizard of Oz*, Baum
   c. *The 120 Days of Sodom*, de Sade
   e. *The Godfather*, Puzo

4. Mrs. Calvi has said her husband was murdered by:
   a. the P2 lodge
   b. the Vatican
   c. the Gnomes of Zurich
   d. the Elders of Zion

5. In 1976 investigating magistrate Vittorio Occorsio began examining the affairs of the P2 Freemasons. Within weeks, he was:
   a. appointed Ambassador to Tasmania and ordered to leave at once to take up his duties there
   b. offered a $1,000,000 bribe by Roberto Calvi
   c. removed to a rest home, uttering weak cries of "It's too complicated… it's too complicated…"
   d. shot dead by machine gun

6. Licio Gelli, Calvi's grandmaster in the P2 lodge, was during World War II:
   a. a member of the Nazi S.S.
   b. a member of a Communist resistance organization
   c. simultaneously a member of the S.S. and of the Communist resistance
   d. an importer of Ethiopian slave-girls for Mussolini's harem

7. According to American journalist Penny Lernoux, Licio

Gelli was employed by the CIA to influence the Italian labour union movement toward the Right and away from the Left. She says he did this by:

    a. placing glossy full-page ads on the virtues of Capitalism in leading Italian newspapers

    b. persuading Sophia Loren to appear in more comedies and less depressing dramas about slum life

    c. bribing union officials

    d. bribing such union officials as could be bribed and hiring Mafia killers to assassinate the others

8. While working for the CIA, Gelli also was on the payroll of:

    a. MI6 (British intelligence)

    b. the KGB

    c. a spaghetti factory in Naples

    d. Playboy Clubs International

9. Licio Gelli was a guest at:

    a. the inauguration party of President Richard Nixon

    b. the inauguration party of President Ronald Reagan

    c. the opening of the first McDonald's in Palermo

    d. the 1978 Halloween cluster-fuck at the Playboy Mansion

10. In the Freemasonic 32° initiation the candidate is exhorted to eternal hostility to one group which is denounced as servitors of "tyranny and superstition". That group is:

    a. the Knights of Malta

    b. the Knights of Columbanus

    c. the Council of Cardinals

    d. the Cult of Cthulhu

11. Which of the following has Licio Gelli *not* been

accused of?
    a. plotting a fascist coup in Italy
    b. illegally selling arms to the government of Israel
    c. illegally selling arms to the government of Argentina
    d. illegally selling arms to the Provisional Irish Republican Army
    e. conspiring in several murders and terrorist bombings
    f. collaborating with Calvi and Archbishop Marcinkus in "laundering" heroin money from both the Mafia and the terrorist Turkish group called the Grey Wolves
    g. helping ex-Nazis escape to South America
    h. ghostwriting Ronald Reagan's speeches

12. When the Italian police raided Gelli's home they found a list of P2 members he had infiltrated into the Italian government. The number of persons on that list was:
    a. 33
    b. 133
    c. 400
    d. 953
    e. 2,023

13. In addition to Calvi and Gelli, which of the following have been Freemasons?
    a. Theobold Wolfe Tone
    b. Mozart
    c. Pope Pius IX
    d. Franklin D. Roosevelt
    e. Rudyard Kipling
    f. J. Edgar Hoover
    g. Benjamin Franklin
    h. Voltaire
    i. Isaac Butt
    j. Adlai Stevenson

k. Neil Armstrong, the first man on the moon

14. According to Freemasonic tradition, the secret name of God is:
   a. Yahweh
   b. Jehovah
   c. Cthulhu
   d. Baphomet
   e. Jah-Bul-On
   f. Shiela-na-Gig

15. The largest Freemasonic order in Switzerland is the Grand Loge Alpina. According to Swiss journalist Mathieu Paoli, the Grand Loge Alpina:
   a. helped Gelli escape from a Swiss jail in August 1983
   b. owns most of the banks in Switzerland
   c. distributes the mystical publications of the mysterious Priory of Sion
   d. demands visual proof that members are uncircumcised before initiating them

16. The American industrialist Henry Ford was convinced the world was secretly run by:
   a. the Elders of Zion
   b. the Priory of Sion
   c. 33° Freemasons
   d. six-foot rabbits from another planet

17. *Le Serpent Rouge* (The Red Serpent) is a pamphlet that allegedly reveals the inner secrets of the Priory of Sion. The week it was published:
   a. President De Gaulle had a heart attack
   b. all three authors were found hanged
   c. all three authors were found hanged with their pockets full of bricks like Roberto Calvi
   d. President Richard Nixon resigned

18. After journalist Mathieu Paoli wrote a book denouncing the Priory of Sion as a serious conspiracy within the de Gaulle government he was:
  a. found hanged with his pockets full of bricks
  b. hired to write thrillers for Hollywood
  c. shot to death while in Israel
  d. exposed as a KGB agent and disappeared

19. Which of the following is a member of the Priory of Sion, according to an exposé by Jean Delaude?
  a. Archbishop Lefebvre
  b. Archbishop Marcinkus
  c. Abbe Ducaud-Bourget
  d. J.G. Ballard

20. Which of the following were or are members of the Priory of Sion, according to *Holy Blood, Holy Grail* by Lincoln, Baigent and Leigh?
  a. Isaac Newton
  b. Piere Plantard de St. Clair
  c. Pope John XXIII
  d. Jean Cocteau

21. On 20 February 1967 the body of Fakhar ul Islam was found beheaded near Melun, France. According to a pamphlet by Henri

Lobineau:

    a. Fakhar ul Islam had been carrying counterfeit stocks stolen from Banco Ambrosiano

    b. Fakhar ul Islam had been carrying secret papers concerning the Priory of Sion

    c. Fakhar ul Islam was a member of the Grey Wolves heroin smuggling ring

    d. Fakhar uk Islam was an industrial spy hired by Pepsi Cola to learn the secret formula of Coca-Cola

Photo: Yoshi Yubai

22. According to the French magazine *Bonne Soiree*, the 23rd Grandmaster of the Priory of Sion was:
    a. Pope John XXIII
    b. Charles de Gaulle
    c. Walt Disney
    d. Jean Cocteau

23. According to *Holy Blood, Holy Grail* which of the following were or are descendants of Jesus Christ and Mary Magdalene?
    a. Bonnie Prince Charlie
    b. Prince Bernhard of the Netherlands
    c. Dr Otto von Hapsburg
    d. Greta Garbo

24. Whatever their affiliation with Jesus and Mary Magdalene, Prince Bernhard and Dr von Hapsburg are members of the secret society called:
    a. the Independent Order of Odd Fellows
    b. the Hamburgers
    c. the Bilderbergers
    d. the Paretheo-Anemetamnytikhood of Eris Esoteric

25. French occultist Gérard de Sède claims there are extraterrestrial supermen living among us, passing as humans. According to *Holy Blood, Holy Grail*, de Sede is:
    a. "the most outrageous fraud and humbug since Cagliostro"
    b. in charge of CIA "disinformation" and "propaganda" in France
    c. himself an extraterrestrial superman
    d. a front man for the Priory of Sion

26. Part of the profits from the film of *The Godfather* went to:
    a. Michele Sindona

b. Roberto Calvi
c. the Vatican Bank
d. a home for the hopelessly perplexed

27. When P2 member Michele Sindona was manager of
Vatican finances in the US he acquired for the Vatican
Bank major holdings in:
a. Procter & Gamble
b. Chase Manhattan Bank
c. the World Trade Center
d. the Franklin National Bank, from which he,
Sindona, had already embezzled $55 million and
left near bankruptcy

28. According to American right-wing publications,
Procter & Gamble:
a. has been infiltrated by the KGB
b. secretly owns a studio where pornographic
movies are made
c. secretly financed the publication of *Ulysses*
d. is owned by Satanists

29. P2 member Michele Sindona has been convicted in
the US of:
a. 28 traffic violations
b. 2 counts of perjury
c. 25 counts of stock and currency fraud
d. 65 counts of fraud, conspiracy, perjury and
faking his own kidnapping to escape persecution

30. Sindona started his career as lawyer for the Mafia's:
a. Cambino and Inzerillo families
b. Casper and Giumbini families
c. Mozzarella and Fongula families
d. Gonorrhea and Hernia families

31. According to David Yallop, Licio Gelli, in addition to

his other affiliations was:
 a. a Knight of Columbanus
 b. a secret lover of Sophia Loren
 c. cocaine supplier for Sid Vicious

32. "The Knights of Columbanus are nefarious but not criminal" was said by:
 a. Pope John XXIII
 b. Sean MacBride
 c. Pope John Paul I
 d. Voltaire

33. According to Mrs. Calvi, the Vatican Bank, left in financial distress after Calvi's death and Banco Ambrosiano's collapse, was rescued by a huge donation from which secret society?
 a. the Ordo Templi Orientis
 b. the Knights of Columbanus
 c. Opus Dei
 d. the Knights of the Rose Croix

34. According to New York District Attorney Frank Hogan, the Mafia printed one billion dollars in counterfeit stocks in 1972. This huge counterfeiting project was commissioned by:
 a. the CIA
 b. President Richard Nixon personally
 c. the Priory of Sion
 d. Cardinal Tisserant and Archbishop Marcinkus

35. According to Joseph Coffey, detective on Hogan's staff, after the printers of the billion dollars in counterfeit stock were arrested, Hogan was prevented from pursuing those who commissioned the counterfeiting. The pressure on Hogan came from:
 a. the CIA
 b. President Nixon personally

c. Mysterious men in black who made Freemasonic signs when talking to Hogan

d. Officers in charge of the Air Force's UFO investigation

36. A scientific voice-stress analysis commissioned by *Penthouse* magazine determined that when Lee Harvey Oswald told reporters "I never shot anybody, I'm just the patsy," he was:

a. under the influence of drugs

b. clinically insane

c. lying

d. telling the truth

37. There have bee a series of mysterious cattle mutilations in the U.S. since 1968. Various theorists have attributed these to:

a. a Satanist cult

b. UFOs

c. CIA attempts to cover up chemical warfare experiments

d. giant Killer Rabbits of the same mutant strain as the one that attacked President Carter in August 1979

38. A great deal has been published in the U.S. about "the men in black." They are:

a. the CIA's poison department

b. two men seen on the Grassy Knoll in Dealey Plaza when Kennedy was shot

c. three men seen entering and leaving the Vatican the night Pope John Paul I died

d. "Oriental-looking" persons who frequently threaten and harass citizens who have reported UFOs

39. Jacques Vallée is one of the few astronomers who has

reported seeing a UFO. According to Dr. Vallée, UFOs are probably:
    a. spaceships from another galaxy
    b. time-travelers from the future
    c. angels
    d. a "mind-control" experiment by a government intelligence agency as a "cover" for other mind-control projects

40. According to Father Malachi Martin, Pope John Paul I received from Archbishop Lefebvre, shortly before his (the Pope's) death:
    a. a list of Freemasons in the Vatican
    b. photos of Cardinals with their girl-friends
    c. photos of Cardinals with their boy-friends
    d. Sophia Loren's unlisted phone number

41. The Freemasonic lodge which has historically been suspected of even more crimes than P2 is the Order of the Illuminati. This was founded:
    a. in 1073 by Jacques de Molay
    b. in 1776 by Adam Weishaupt
    c. in 1913 by Baron Rothschild
    d. in 1952 as a CIA "deep cover" operation

42. Like Licio Gelli, who worked for secret groups opposed to each other, the English occultist Aleister Crowley worked for both British and German intelligence in World War I. Crowley was also:
    a. a 33° Freemason
    b. Grandmaster of the Priory of Sion
    c. Epopt of the Illuminati
    d. Outer Head of the Ordo Templi Orientis
    e. Bishop of the Gnostic Catholic Church

43. Orthodox (Accepted) Freemasonry has 33 degrees. The Ordo Templi Orientis admits to only 10 degrees. The

secret 11th degree of the Ordo Templi Orientis is reserved for:
   a. relatives of David Rockefeller
   b. members of the Rothschild family
   c. the extraterrestrial supermen alleged by Gérard de Sède
   d. homosexuals

44. According to Freemasonic tradition, when Solomon heard of the death of Hiram he said:
   a. "The rosewater of Lebanon hath turned to urine and the Lily of Shiloh is as a pile of elephant manure."
   b. "Hide the evidence and say it was a heart attack."
   c. "Sacrilegious murder hath made his masterpiece."
   d. "O Lord my God is there no hope for the widow's son?"

45. Father Bérgener Saunière, of the small parish of Rennes-le-Château in France, has become the subject of much conspiratorial speculation because he:
   a. went to investigate a UFO sighting and was never seen again
   b. became very rich by unknown means
   c. was an associate of the Hermetic Brotherhood of Light in Paris
   d. once bragged, when drunk, that he had forged the Casement diaries for MI5

46. Father Saunière built a church to Mary Magdalene in Rennes-le-Château. Over the door he inscribed the words:
   a. "Non Illegitimati Carborundum"
   b. "The Kingdom of Heaven is Within"
   c. "No Popery"
   d. "This Place is Terrible"

47. According to Michael Lamy's *Jules Verne, Initiate et*

Initateur, Verne was:
    a. secret financial advisor to the Rothschilds
    b. member of the Illuminati and associate of Father Saunière
    c. a Tibetan Buddhist masquerading as a Frenchman
    d. one of the superhuman extraterrestrials alleged by de Sède

48. When Juan Peron was restored to power in Argentina he knelt publicly and gave thanks to:
    a. the Blessed Virgin Mary
    b. St. Jude
    c. David Rockefeller
    d. Licio Gelli

49. [missing!]

50. Which of the following were NOT business associates of Licio Gelli:
    a. Archbishop Marcinkus
    b. Roberto Calvi
    c. Klaus Barbie
    d. Michele Sindona
    e. J. Paul Getty
    f. Guillermo Hernández-Cartaya

51. "Odessa" is:
    a. a fictitious conspiracy in a thriller by Frederick Forsyth
    b. a code-name for a CIA "mole" in the KGB
    c. the organization of fugitive Nazi war criminals that, working with P2, helped organize the death squads in Latin America
    d. a tranquilizer that had to be removed from the market when it was found to have aphrodisiac side-effects

52. Both the Trilateral Commission and the Bilderbergers have been suspect in some quarters because they are largely financed by David Rockefeller of Chase Manhattan Bank. Which of the following are NOT members of both the Trilateral Commission and the Bilderbergers?
a. Henry Kissinger
b. Prince Bernhard of the Netherlands
c. Archbishop Marcinkus
d. Garret FitzGerald, Prime Minister of Ireland

53. Former U.S. President Gerald Ford:
a. was a 33° Freemason and a member of the Bilderbergers
b. was a 33° Freemason and a member of the Priory of Sion
c. was J. Edgar Hoover's spy in the Warren Commission investigation of the John Kennedy assassination
d. granted a Presidential pardon to Richard Nixon for all crimes known or later to be discovered

54. Rockefeller's Chase Manhattan Bank covered the unsecured loans of the Penn Square Bank in Oklahoma, and took a multi-million-dollar loss when Penn Square went bankrupt. A vice-president of Penn Square, William Patterson, had the odd habit of:
a. wearing Mickey Mouse ears to the office
b. flying to Rome for weekly conferences with Archbishop Marcinkus
c. smoking cannabis during lunch hour
d. asking customers if they knew a four-letter word meaning "intercourse" ending with "k," and then telling them it was "talk," while laughing insanely

55. The World Finance Corporation of Miami, Florida, came to the attention of the local District Attorney when:
a. neighbors reported frequent UFO landings in the

bank's parking lot

b. customers complained the clerks continually cheated them

c. an informer told police the bank was a Mafia front

d. garbage collectors told police they found cannabis stems and seeds in the trash

56. On Investigation, the District Attorney concluded that World Finance Corporation was:

a. the biggest-scale Mafia "laundromat" for drug money ever uncovered

b. the principal bank for Latin American governments involved in the cocaine trade

c. involved in illegal transactions with the Cisalpine Bank in the Bahamas

d. a funnel for "deep cover" CIA funds for clandestine operations

57. The Cisalpine Bank, linked to drug-money laundering with Banco Ambrosiano and others, is largely owned by:

a. the Vatican Bank

b. Archbishop Marcinkus personally

c. David Rockefeller

d. Robert Vesco

58. Robert Vesco, major financial backer of Richard Nixon, is wanted in the United States for:

a. molesting women in shopping centers

b. suspicion of murder

c. irregular dealings with the World Finance Corporation

d. defrauding his stock-holders of several hundred million dollars

59. The CIA once managed to place a mole in the Russian Embassy in Washington. His code name was:

a. Tricycle
b. the Red Queen
c. Fedora
d. Bugs Bunny

60. When the CIA mole in the Russian Embassy in Washington was discovered to be a KGB officer deliberately deceiving his CIA contacts, he:
a. was ordered to leave the U.S. in 24 hours
b. was arrested and then traded for an American agent imprisoned in Russia
c. was found hanged with his pockets full of bricks
d. flew back to Moscow before any CIA action could be taken

61. Mattieu Paoli found the journal of the Priory of Sion, *CIRCUIT*, was published out of:
a. a seemingly deserted warehouse in Milan
b. Procter & Gamble's publicity department
c. the Zurich office of Cisalpine Bank
d. the government office of the French Committee for Public Safety in Paris

62. Guillermo Hernández-Cartaya, president of the World Finance Corporation "drug laundromat" was previously:
a. an associate of E. Howard Hunt in the Bay of Pigs invasion
b. one of the Cubans involved in the Watergate burglary
c. Elizabeth Taylor's sixth husband
d. Godfather to two of David Rockefeller's children

63. When E. Howard Hunt threatened to "spill the whole Bay of Pigs thing" President Nixon:
a. hired assassins to kill Hunt
b. resigned from office
c. agreed to pay Hunt $1,000,000

Photo: Yoshi Yubai

d. went on television to make a speech about his dog, Checkers

64. When Mrs. Hunt was killed in a plane crash while carrying $100,000 in bribe money from Nixon, the pilot was found at the inquest to have:

a. a previous history of manic-depressive psychosis

b. an astonishing resemblance to the "second Oswald" in Dallas

c. a membership card in the King Kong Died For You Society

d. 3.9 micrograms per milliliter of cyanide in his blood

65. Gordon Thomas claims Pope John Paul II has secret weekly meetings with:

a. Joan Collins

b. Senior CIA officials in Rome

c. a psychotherapist

d. the Ayatollah Khomeini

66. Mafioso Johnny Roselli:

a. was involved in the 1972 billion-dollar counterfeit stock swindle

b. was accused of complicity in the John Kennedy assassination

c. told columnist Jack Anderson that another Mafia family WAS involved in the Kennedy assassination

d. was shot to death while under investigation by the U.S. Justice Department

67. General Santovito, head of SISMI (the Italian secret police) during P2's infiltration of the Italian government:

a. was so humiliated when the scandals broke that he resigned his post and entered a monastery to do Penance

b. was sacked after evidence proved he was also a

P2 member

c. was found hanged with his pockets full of bricks

d. was the brother-in-law of Pope John Paul I

68. General Musumeci, deputy chief of SISMI under General Santovito:

a. is now fearlessly pursuing an investigation of the rest of the P2 group

b. fell or was pushed out of a window in Rome in July 1984

c. is now under indictment for plotting, with P2 leaders, the 1980 Bologna bombing in which 20 were killed and 80 injured

d. was Licio Gelli's brother-in-law

69. Calls to ban Freemasons from the Ulster police were made in September 1984 by:

a. SDLP Deputy Leader Seamus Mallon

b. DUP Assemblyman Rev. Ivan Foster

c. Gerry Adams

d. Rev. Ian Paisley

70. David Ferrie, the first man indicted by New Orleans District Attorney Jim Garrison for conspiracy in the John Kennedy assassination:

a. died within hours after the indictment of a karate chop to the neck

b. disappeared and has never been seen again

c. seems to be standing next to Licio Gelli in a recent photo of Gelli in his Uruguay hide-out

d. was acquitted by the jury and later became a hair stylist in Hollywood

71. David Ferrie was a former CIA agent and a priest of the Old Catholic Church. The Old Catholic Church differs from the Roman Catholic church principally in that:

a. it does not recognize Papal infallibility

b. it claims there are four, not three, persons in one God

c. all of its priests are admitted homosexuals

d. it recognizes the Bible and the Necronomicon as equally sacred

72. The second man indicted in Garrison's assassination investigation, Gordon Brownell, fled to Arlington, Virginia, and resisted extradition back to New Orleans. Coincidentally, Arlington was then:

    a. the headquarters of the CIA

    b. the headquarters of the American Nazi Party

    c. the home of E. Howard Hunt

    d. the headquarters of the First Church of Satan

73. In September 1984 Paddy James of Dunnes Stores Group told a committee of the Irish Senate that:

    a. Prime Minister Garret FitzGerald had tried to recruit him into the Bilderbergers

    b. Garret FitzGerald has tried to recruit him into the Priory of Sion

    c. the Freemasons had put pressure on Dunnes to buy non-Irish-made products

    d. the current Irish government are "damned ijjits"

74. Stephen Knight in *The Brotherhood* alleges that:

    a. Roberto Calvi was murdered by P2 Freemasons and the crime covered up by a cabal of Freemasons in Scotland Yard

    b. the Knights of Malta have murdered over 80 people in attempts to recover the "Maltese Falcon"

    c. Freemasons are favored for promotion in Scotland Yard

    d. the Bugs Bunny cartoons are "an insidious form of Freemasonic" propaganda

75. In *Jack the Ripper, the Final Solution,* Knight also

alleges that:
> a. the Ripper murders were also covered up by a Freemasonic cabal in Scotland Yard
> b. The Ripper murders were committed by Queen Victoria's grandson, the Duke of Clarence
> c. "Jack the Ripper" was actually three different men
> d. the purpose of the Ripper murders was to cover up evidence of an Irish Catholic heir to the British throne

76. According to the *Irish Press* for 5 September 1984, the number of Freemasons in Scotland Yard is:
> a. seven
> b. about 30
> c. more than 50
> d. "hundreds"

77. "The history of the world is the history of the warfare of secret societies" was said by:
> a. Machiavelli
> b. Stephen Knight
> c. Adolph Hitler
> d. American novelist Ishmael Reed

78. When Bismarck tried to provoke war with France in 1872 by making impossible demands on the French government, they surprised him by accepting his terms. He then:
> a. shrugged and decided not to have a war that year after all
> b. got drunk for two weeks
> c. concealed the French documents and declared war anyway
> d. hired Mafia assassins to poison Louis Napoleon

79. According to U.S. historian Harry Elmer Barnes, on 1

December 1941, President Roosevelt:
 a. ordered a U.S. ship sent into the path of the
 Japanese task force to draw their fire
 b. sent obscene and insulting limericks to Emperor
 Hirohito
 c. trained his dog, Fala, to pee on the leg of the
 Japanese Ambassador every time he saw him
 d. heatedly demanded that Alger Hiss notify
 the military authorities in Pearl Harbor of the
 impending Japanese attack

80. U.S. intelligence cracked the Japanese diplomatic code in 1940. The information indicating the impending attack on U.S. forces was withheld from:
 a. President Roosevelt by KGB moles in the U.S.
 State Department
 b. the American people
 c. the military commanders at Pearl Harbor
 d. J. Edgar Hoover because Roosevelt considered
 him "a blabbermouth"

81. The Gulf of Tonkin resolution by the U.S. Congress permitted President Johnson to vastly increase U.S. troops in Vietnam. It was written:
 a. within hours after North Vietnamese fired on an
 American ship
 b. two days after the firing on the American ship
 c. a week after the firing on the American ship
 d. weeks BEFORE the firing on the American ship

82. Every Tarot deck has a card called The Hanged Man. The only deck in which the Hanged Man is submerged in water like Roberto Calvi is:
 a. the Marseilles Tarot
 b. the Arthur Waite Tarot
 c. the Walt Disney Tarot
 d. the Aleister Crowley Tarot

83. "Papus" was an associate of the mysterious Father Saunière and Bishop of the Gnostic Catholic Church. The real name of "Papus" was:
   a. Jules Verne
   b. Gerard Encause
   c. Jean Cocteau
   d. Brian O'Nolan

84. The Order of the Illuminati was revived in 1888 by:
   a. "Papus" and Aleister Crowley
   b. Marx and Engels
   c. Leopold Engels
   d. Leopold Bloom

85. After appointing Aleister Crowley his successor as Bishop of the Gnostic Catholic Church, "Papus":
   a. left the room abruptly and had a laughing fit for two hours
   b. went to Milan and became a director of Banco Ambrosiano
   c. went to the United States and became Woodrow Wilson's astrologer
   d. went to Russia and became an associate of Rasputin

86. The "Bible" of the Ku Klux Klan is called:
   a. the Koran
   b. the Kloran
   c. the Necronomicon
   d. the Ku Klux Katechism

87. The password and counter-pass of the Ku Klux Klan:
   a. "No Popery"/"No Dopery"
   b. "No Popery"/"No Race Mixing"
   c. "White Man"/"Native Born"
   d. "What's up, Doc?"/"You rascal rabbit"

88. "Are you a trull?" "You bet your sweet ass I am!" is the password and counter-pass of:
    a. the Ancient Order of Hibernians
    b. the American branch of P2
    c. an informal association of airline pilots
    d. the Ancient and Mystical Order of the Rosæ Crucis (AMORC)

89. "The guardian at noon blue apples" is part of:
    a. a parchment allegedly found by Father Saunière which de Sède interprets as a code concerning extraterrestrials
    b. Chapter Four of *Finnegans Wake*
    c. a burlesque of Freemasonic initiations used by the Independent Order of Odd Fellows
    d. the Egyptian *Book of the Dead*

90. "It rains" is:
    a. another part of the alleged Father Saunière parchments
    b. Freemasonic code, meaning there are non-Freemasons in the room
    c. the last words of Beethoven
    d. the last line of Beckett's *Malone Dies*

91. "Peace 681 by the Cross and this horse of God" is:
    a. another part of the alleged Father Saunière parchments
    b. the last words of Pope John Paul I
    c. part of an aleatoric poem by Tristan Tzara
    d. part of the coded telegram sent by Roosevelt to Churchill on 7 December 1941

92. "A boy has never wept nor dashed a thousand kim" is:
    a. another part of the Father Saunière parchments
    b. Freemasonic mnemonic for the Names of Power [Asmodeus, Belial, Hastur, Nyarlathotep, Wotan,

Nemo, Diabolo, Azathoth, Thor, Kali]
c. part of the last words of American gangster,
Dutch Schultz
d. gibberish we just invented to confuse our readers

93. "The comedy is finished" is:
a. the last words of the Freemasonic 10° initiation
b. the last words of Shakespeare's *Titus Andronicus*
c. the last words of Aleister Crowley's Gnostic
Catholic Mass
d. the last words of Beethoven

94. During the entire term of office of President Franklin
Roosevelt (1933-45) all U.S. newspapers collaborated in
hiding from the public that:
a. actress Fay Wray was Roosevelt's mistress
b. the president's wife was part-Negro
c. Roosevelt and Churchill were half-brothers,
Roosevelt being Randolph Churchill's natural son
by Lillian Gish
d. Roosevelt was a cripple in a wheelchair

95. According to Deirdre Manifold's *Fatima and the Great
Conspiracy,* the three principal villains of Western history
have been:
a. Martin Luther, Adam Weishaupt and Garret
FitzGerald
b. Martin Luther, Adam Weishaupt and Paterson,
the founder of the Bank of England
c. Karl Marx, Groucho Marx and Mark Twain
d. Karl Marx, V.I. Lenin and James Connolly

96. The Hermetic order of the Golden Dawn is an
irregular Freemasonic lodge founded by MacGregor
Mathers. Mathers alleged that he:
a. was a direct descendant of Bonnie Prince Charlie
b. was in communication with extraterrestrial

superhumans

c. was in communication with undefined superhumans

d. was able to project his astral body as far as the moon

97. Which of the following were NOT members of the Hermetic Order of the Golden Dawn?

    a. William Butler Yeats

    b. Aleister Crowley

    c. Sean O'Casey

    d. Winston Churchill

98. Adolph Hitler told Hermann Rauschning that the Superman:

    a. would be produced after 1000 years of scientific breeding

    b. is "a useful myth to befuddle the idiots"

    c. "is among us now. I have met him."

    d. "was MY idea, and the Americans have stolen it for their silly comic books, and I will see that they are punished."

99. Helena Blavatsky, founder of the Theosophical Society, claimed to be in contact with a superhuman being called:

    a. Koot-Hoomi

    b. Cthulhu

    c. Coot Jackson

    d. Coot-An-Fern

100. Aleister Crowley said the only recent Europeans to attain his degree of spiritual enlightenment were:

    a. Helena Blavatsky and Adam Weishaupt

    b. William Butler Yeats and Carl Jung

    c. William Butler Yeats and James Joyce

    d. William Blake and Adam Weishaupt

101. According to Christina Stoddard's *The Trail of the Serpent,* virtually every secret society in the world has been:
    a. infiltrated by agents of British intelligence
    b. infiltrated by the Illuminati
    c. infiltrated by the KGB
    d. infiltrated by the CIA

102. According to Pauwels and Bergier in *The Morning of the Magicians,* Hitler joined a secret society in 1923. It was called:
    a. the Cthulhu Society
    b. the Thule Society
    c. the Knights of Malta
    d. the Order of the Peacock Angel

103. Which of the following was NOT used by the CIA in attempts to assassinate Fidel Castro?
    a. poisoned cigar
    b. explosive sea-shell
    c. contaminated diving suit
    d. poisoned ballpoint pen
    e. professional Mafia assassins
    f. poisoned bananas

104. "You can't run a church on Hail Marys" was said by:
    a. Machiavelli
    b. Voltaire
    c. Lord Acton
    d. Archbishop Marcinkus

105. The Ordo Templi Orientis is another irregular Freemasonic lodge that has aroused conspiratorial speculation. When Theodor Reuss was Outer Head of the Ordo Templi Orientis he was also:
    a. the largest cocaine dealer in Berlin
    b. an agent of German intelligence, assigned to

Photo: Yoshi Yubai

befriend and spy on Karl Marx
c. ghost-writing *The Communist Manifesto* for Marx
d. composing most of the obscene limericks that are
still in circulation

106. Members of the Ordo Templi Orientis use special
mental exercises to contact a being called AIWASS. When
Aleister Crowley was Outer Head of the OTO, he told an
American disciple that AIWASS was:
a. a 1000-year-old being living on a planet of the
star, Sirius
b. "my superior in MI5 in London"
c. Satan
d. "your own unconscious mind"

107. The "Twenty Bureau" of British intelligence is or
was in charge of:
a. investigating counterfeit £20 notes
b. managing the Ordo Templi Orientis
c. recruiting or coercing enemy agents to work for
British intelligence
d. infiltrating the I.R.A.

108. The difference between MI5 and MI6 is that:
a. only 33° Freemasons are admitted to MI5
b. MI5 seeks to discover agents of foreign powers
in England, while MI6 manages English agents in
other countries
c. all known or suspected homosexuals are assigned
to MI6
d. the Prime Minister is informed of MI5 projects
but only God knows what MI6 is doing

109. In the private argot of the CIA "useful idiot" means:
a. an agent for MI5
b. whoever is president of the U.S. at the time
c. a member of the Bilderbergers

d. a person working for them, through a front, but unaware of it

110. The CIA owns explicit films, made with hidden cameras, of the sexual adventures of:
a. Martin Luther King Jr.
b. every U.S. president since Truman
c. Joan Collins
d. President Sukarno

111. Hitler ordered the suppression of all ordinary Freemasonic lodges in Germany but members of Ordo Templi Orientis lodges were:
a. allowed to go on operating and, if possible, recruited for the S.S.
b. placed under 24-hour-a-day Gestapo surveillance
c. arrested and sent to concentration camps
d. sterilized

112. During the 1° initiation for the Ordo Templi Orientis, candidates must sign a statement of principles. This ends with the sentence:
a. "Death to the Pope!"
b. "There is no God but Jehovah."
c. "There is no God but Allah."
d. "There is no god but Man."

113. The motto of the medieval Order of Assassins was:
a. "Truth is many, but men have one name for it."
b. "Nothing is true; all is permissible."
c. "Kill for the love of Kali!"
d. "Truth is one, but men have many names for it."

114. A month before he shot Robert Kennedy, Sirhan Sirhan wrote to the Ancient and Mystical Order of the Rosæ Crucis (AMORC) asking:
a. the correct techniques for astral projection

b. if members of AMORC have to accept the Rose Cross initiation of Freemasonry

c. if Rosicrucianism cures sexual inadequacy

d. how to contact the Order of the Illuminati

115. Mehmet Ali Agca, who tried to assassinate Pope John Paul II, was:

a. a member of the "Grey Wolves" heroin-smuggling ring

b. second cousin to Sirhan Sirhan

c. an agent of the Bulgarian secret police, according to Italian investigating magistrates

d. brainwashed by the CIA, according to Bulgarian government spokesmen

116. Eccentric millionaire Howard Hughes was convinced David Rockefeller:

a. was using the Trilateral Commission to take over the world

b. was plotting to take Hughes Aircraft away from him

c. was behind both of the Kennedy assassinations

d. was the Great Beast foretold in St. John's *Revelations*

117. According to historian Carl Oglesby, Hughes fought back against Rockefeller by giving bribes to:

a. President Nixon's brother, Donald

b. 20 Congressmen

c. the Securities and Exchange Commission

d. Nixon's brother and everybody in Congress, the Senate, or any of the 50 State legislatures that would take a bribe

118. After Hughes donated $150,000 to Nixon's 1972 election campaign, Nixon's private espionage group, "the Plumbers,"

a. went to Las Vegas and had a party with Hughes
b. went to Las Vegas for purposes that have been disclosed
c. went to Las Vegas and, while they were there, a newspaper was burglarized
d. installed a wiretap on David Rockefeller

119. The CIA dossier on Aleister Crowley is marked:
a. "Not to be removed from this building"
b. "Mind control, a, II, ref 56"
c. "Nut file"
d. "To be used with extreme caution"

120. According to Col. Thomas Bearden's *Excalibur Briefing,* the KGB:
a. secretly finances Procter & Gamble
b. murdered Pope John Paul I
c. murdered Marilyn Monroe
d. employs psychics to control Western politicians by telepathy

121. Howard Hughes placed the following actresses under surveillance:
a. Sophia Loren
b. Anne Bancroft
c. Elizabeth Taylor
d. Jane Russell

122. Industrialist Henry Ford believed E.I. du Pont de Nemours & Co.:
a. were trying to kill him with poisoned bananas
b. were putting heroin in his tea to make him an addict
c. always picked both the Republican and Democratic candidates for president
d. murdered two industrial spies he had infiltrated into their management

Photo: Yoshi Yubai

123. According to Stephen Knight, the KGB:
a. has infiltrated British Freemasonic lodges
b. has infiltrated British intelligence services
c. managed the P2 conspiracy in Italy
d. put heroin in Henry Ford's tea to make him an addict

124. Around the Vatican, Archbishop Marcinkis is nicknamed:
a. Goldfinger
b. Moneybags
c. the Red Queen
d. the Gorilla

125. The current Grandmaster of all Freemasons in the U.K. and Ireland is:
a. the Archbishop of Canterbury
b. the Duke of Kent
c. the Lord of Howth
d. John Cleese

126. According to Gordon Thomas, Pope John Paul II and the CIA communicate via:
a. a high orbit radio satellite
b. mental telepathy
c. ordinary mail
d. the Knights of Malta, who act as couriers

127. In Penny Lernoux's *In Banks We Trust,* which of the following banks is NOT accused of laundering drug money?
a. the World Finance Corporation
b. the Cisalpine Bank
c. Chase Manhattan Bank
d. the Vatican Bank
e. Banco Ambrosiano
f. the Nugan Hand Bank of Australia

g. the Bank of Ireland

128. Pope John Paul XXIII has been accused of being a Freemason by:
a. Father Malachi Martin
b. Archbishop Lefebvre
c. Gérard de Sède
d. the authors of *Holy Blood, Holy Grail*

129. Father Juan Krohn, who tried to assassinate Pope John Paul II at Fatima, was ordained by:
a. Archbishop Marcinkus
b. Archbishop Lefebvre
c. Archbishop Cody
d. Archbishop Benelli

130. "Conspiracy is the normal continuation of normal politics by normal means" was said by:
a. Machiavelli
b. Licio Gelli
c. Theobold Wolfe Tone
d. Historian Carl Oglesby

131. J. Edgar Hoover made FBI tapes of Martin Luther King's sexual adventures available to:
a. the five other 33° Freemasons in Washington
b. the Boy Scouts of America, for sex education courses
c. President Lyndon Johnson, who played them for his friends
d. Archbishop Cody of Chicago

132. "There is one dangerous element in Freemasory and that is what I have copied from them" was said by:
a. St. Ignatius Loyola
b. Rev. Sun Myung Moon
c. Charlie Manson

d. Adolph Hitler

133. In the Watergate transcripts, President Nixon said J. Edgar Hoover had a file on:
    a. all the homosexuals in Washington
    b. all the cannabis dealers in Orange, New Jersey
    c. John Kennedy's love affair with Marilyn Monroe
    d. everybody

134. Which of the following has NOT been alleged to have infiltrated the Vatican?
    a. the P2 Freemasons
    b. the orthodox or "Accepted" Freemasons
    c. the Priory of Sion
    d. the Cthulhu Cult

135. "Anybody in Washington who isn't paranoid must be crazy" was said by:
    a. Richard Nixon
    b. Ronald Reagan
    c. Henry Kissinger
    d. G. Gordon Liddy

136. In September 1978 Pope John Paul I was sent (by *Osservatore Polico*) a list of alleged Freemasons in the Vatican. The list contained:
    a. 15 names
    b. 50 names
    c. 90 names
    d. 121 names

137. Pope John Paul I requested Cardinal Villot to investigate the actual extent of Freemasons in the Vatican. Cardinal Villot's investigation:
    a. proved there were no Freemasons in the Vatican
    b. found two real Freemasons, who were removed

and excommunicated
c. found three Freemasons, who were so brilliant
in administration that the Pope decided to forgive
them and keep them in their positions
d. has never been heard of again

138. According to David Yallop's *In God's Name,* lodge
number 041/3 in a Zurich Freemasonic lodge belongs to:
    a. Licio Gelli
    b. Roberto Calvi
    c. the Prince of Wales
    d. Cardinal Villot

139. Mino Pecorelli, editor/publisher of *Osservatore
Politico,* who sent the list of alleged Freemasons to Pope
John Paul I, subsequently:
    a. admitted that it had been a hoax and vowed to do
    5 years penance
    b. fell or was pushed out of his office window
    c. was found hanged with his pockets full of bricks
    d. was shot to death on the street

140. The death certificate on Pope John Paul I:
    a. gives cause of death as "accidental overdose"
    b. gives cause of death as "heart attack"
    c. gives cause of death as "unknown"
    d. has never been revealed by the Vatican

141. Abbot Ducaud-Bourget said of the death of Pope
John Paul I:
    a. "We all knew the old man had a bad heart"
    b. "It is hard to believe this death was natural"
    c. "There is a time to speak, and a time to be silent"
    d. "I am perplexed"

142. Which of the following items disappeared
mysteriously from Pope John Paul I's bedroom the

morning his body was found?
    a. papers he had been working on
    b. his medicine
    c. his last will
    d. his glasses
    e. his slippers

143. Abbot Ducaud-Bourget is right-hand-man to Archbishop Lefebvre. According to Bonne Soiree magazine, he also:
    a. was Grandmaster of the Priory of Sion in the early 1970s
    b. owns a large share of the Cisalpine Bank
    c. is a member of the Bilderbergers
    d. writes most of Archbishop Lefebvre's speeches

144. Lodge number 20 in the Freemasonic Lodge of Good Hope in Vienna once belonged to:
    a. Emperor Joseph von Habsburg
    b. Wolfgang Amadeus Mozart
    c. Benjamin Franklin
    d. Sir Roger Casement

145. Beaumarchais wrote the original *Barber of Seville*. He
    a. was an agent of the French secret police
    b. was a member of the Grand Orient Lodge of Egyptian Freemasonry
    c. was in charge of clandestine aid to the American revolutionists from the French court
    d. embezzled money from his own bank

146. The "front" for the Grand Orient Lodge of Egyptian Freemasonry was "Count Cagliostro," who claimed to be 3000 years old. According to Colin Wilson:
    a. Cagliostro was definitely an Italian swindler, Giuseppe Balsamo
    b. It has never been proven that Cagliostro and

Balsamo were the same man

c. Cagliostro took his orders directly from the order of the Illuminati

d. Cagliostro had genuine paranormal powers

147. According to American scientist Buckminster Fuller the modern world is ruled by what he calls MMAO. These initials stand for:

a. madness, mischief, anarchy and obscenity

b. the Masons, the Mafia, the Arabs and Opus Dei

c. malfeasance, malpractice, apathy and obsolescence

d. Machiavelli, the Mafia and the Atomic and Oil cartels

148. Mozart's *Magic Flute* is based on:

a. the Freemasonic 1° initiation

b. the secret teachings of the Illuminati

c. the Finn Mac Cool sagas

d. Mozart's fear that Salieri was plotting against him

149. Beethoven's *Emperor Joseph Cantata* was commissioned by:

a. Emperor Joseph's widow

b. the Freemasonic Lodge of Good Hope

c. the Order of the Illuminati

d. a mysterious man in black wearing a face-mask

150. "The Star Spangled Banner" is the U.S. national anthem. The music was originally:

a. written but abandoned incomplete by Beethoven

b. written by Mozart's father, Leopold

c. used to open Freemasonic rituals in London

d. composed by George Washington for Freemasonic meetings in Mount Vernon

151. When Beethoven left Bonn in 1790 he carried with him a letter from the Grandmaster of the Illuminati lodge in Bonn introducing him to:
    a. the Emperor Joseph von Hapsburg
    b. Cagliostro
    c. Robespierre
    d. several prominent Freemasons in Vienna

152. According to Nettl's *Mozart and Masonry*, the structure of the Illuminati is based on:
    a. the medieval Order of Assassins
    b. the Knights Templar
    c. the Knights of Malta
    d. the Society of Jesus

153. Wagner's *Parsifal* is based on:
    a. the Freemasonic "Rose Cross" initiation
    b. poems written by Adam Weishaupt
    c. an ancient Egyptian text
    d. the 9° initiation of the Ordo Templi Orientis

154. The book given a place of honor in all British and American Freemasonic lodges is:
    a. the Koran
    b. the Bible
    c. the Necronomicon
    d. the Egyptian *Book of the Dead*

155. Casanova, in his defense of Freemasonry, admits that:
    a. some Freemasons have been scoundrels
    b. you must conniver with Islam to be a Freemason
    c. some Freemasonic lodges have been infiltrated by political conspirators
    d. "that business with the billy-goat is extremely undignified"

156. Sir John Masterman defined the function of an intelligence service as:
    a. "maintaining peace and national security with minimum fuss and publicity"
    b. "providing make-work for Cambridge intellectuals who have no practical abilities at all"
    c. "maintaining the British Empire by any means necessary"
    d. "taking over the enemy's intelligence network, or as much of it as we can get our hands on"

157. When Voltaire was initiated as a Freemason among those present was:
    a. Cagliostro
    b. Adam Weishaupt
    c. Benjamin Franklin
    d. Marat

158. "Any fool can commit a murder. It takes an artist to arrange a natural death" was said by:
    a. Beria, head of Stalin's secret police
    b. Fouché, head of Napoleon's secret police
    c. the Empress Livia Augusta
    d. G. Gordon Liddy

159. The day Archduke Ferdinand was assassinated in Sarajevo, leading to World War I:
    a. Father Saunière was assassinated in Rennes-le-Chatteau
    b. a second, and seemingly unrelated, assassination attempt on Ferdinand had failed just hours before
    c. the first attempt was made to assassinate Rasputin in Russia
    d. John D. Rockefeller was seen in conference with elderly Zionists

160. "When four sit down to conspire, three are fools and

Photo: Yoshi Yubai

the fourth is a government agent" was said by:
 a. Duncan Lunan
 b. Machiavelli
 c. J. Edgar Hoover
 d. Ian Fleming

161. The airline crash that killed Dorothy Hunt, wife of
E. Howard Hunt, was attributed to the CIA by:
 a. *Pravda*
 b. Jane Fonda
 c. *Playboy* magazine
 d. former Nixon aide, Charles Colson

162. Three "tramps" were arrested on the grassy knoll in
Dealey Plaza after the John Kennedy assassination, but
quickly released. In photographs one of the tramps looks
astonishingly like:
 a. Mafioso Johnny Roselli
 b. E. Howard Hunt
 c. Mayor Daley of Chicago
 d. G. Gordon Liddy

163. In the 1960s the FBI's COINTELPRO operation was
intended to infiltrate peace groups and also:
 a. infiltrate the CIA to inform FBI director and 33°
 Freemason J. Edgar Hoover how many CIA agents
 were Knights of Malta
 b. plant cannabis on peace movement leaders so
 they could be arrested
 c. set off bombs and blame them on pacifists
 d. create paranoia by allowing peace groups to
 discover they were being infiltrated

164. That the Provisional IRA has been infiltrated by
British intelligence has been charged by:
 a. Gerry Adams
 b. Sean MacBride

c. David Yallop

d. Enoch Powell

165. That the Provos have been infiltrated by the CIA has been charged by:

a. *Pravda*

b. Jane Fonda

c. Stephen Knight

d. Enoch Powell

166. "All power tends to corrupt, and absolute power corrupts absolutely" was said by:

a. Lord Acton

b. Thomas Jefferson

c. Edmund Burke

d. Pope Pius IX

167. "Where there is no limit to power, there is no limit to conspiracy" was said by:

a. Lord Acton

b. Historian Edward Gibbon

c. Suetonius

d. Historian Carl Oglesby

168. "Roman Catholicism, Freemasonry and Naziism cannot co-exist. Two of the three must perish" was said by:

a. Pope Pius XII

b. Rudolf Hess

c. Adolph Hitler

d. the Duke of Kent

169. Reinhard Gehlen, head of German Military Intelligence under Hitler:

a. was hanged as a war criminal

b. escaped to South America with Klaus Barbie

c. has never been located

d. became the CIA's top man in Berlin

170. Admiral Canaris, head of Naval Intelligence under Hitler:
    a. was hanged as a war criminal
    b. was last seen in conference with Licio Gelli in Uruguay
    c. was tried as a war criminal but acquitted
    d. was revealed, after his death, to have been working for the British all through World War II

171. Novelist William S. Burroughs says governments using modern mind-control techniques can survive without a police force. But he adds that no government can survive without:
    a. the faith of the people
    b. taxation
    c. "heroic vision"
    d. "bullshit"

172. When questioned about the Vatican Bank's involvement in the crimes of the P2 crowd, Pope John Paul II replied:
    a. "I have ordered a thorough investigation and the guilty will be punished."
    b. "You can't run a church on Hail Marys."
    c. "No spik-a de English"
    d. "Your faith must never be questioned because of what you read in the newspapers."

Photo: Yoshi Yubai

ANSWERS

1. d	31. b	63. c
2. d	32. b	64. d
3. d	33. c	65. b
4. b	34. d	66. a, b, c and d
5. d	35. b	67. b
6. a, b and c	36. d	68. c
7. c and d	37. a, b and c	69. a
8. b	38. d	70. a
9. b	39. d	71. a and c
10. a	40. a, b and c	72. a, b and c
11. d and h	41. b	73. c
12. d	42. a, c, d and e	74. a and c
13. a, b, d, e, f, g, h, i, j and k	43. d	75. a, c and d
	44. d	76. d
14. e	45. b and c	77. d
15. c	46. d	78. c
16. a	47. b	79. a
17. b	48. d	80. b and c
18. c	50. e	81. d
19. a and b	51. c	82. d
20. a, b, c and d	52. c	83. b
21. b	53. a, c and d	84. c
22. d	54. a	85. d
23. a, b and c	55. d	86. b
24. c	56. a, b, c and d	87. c
25. d	57. b	88. c
26. a, b and c	58. d	89. a
27. a, b, c and d	59. c	90. b
28. d	60. d	91. a
29. d	61. d	92. c
30. a	62. a	93. d

94. d
95. b
96. a and c
97. c and d
98. c
99. a
100. a
101. b
102. b
103. f
104. d
105. b
106. d
107. c
108. b
109. d
110. d
111. c
112. d
113. b
114. d
115. a, c and d
116. b
117. a and d
118. b and c
119. d
120. d
121. a, b and d
122. d
123. a, b and c
124. d

125. b
126. d
127. g
128. a, b and d
129. b
130. d
131. c
132. d
133. d
134. d
135. c
136. d
137. d
138. d
139. d
140. d
141. b
142. a, b, c, d, e
143. a
144. b
145. a, b, c and d
146. b and d
147. d
148. a
149. c
150. c
151. d
152. d
153. d
154. b
155. c

156. d
157. c
158. a
159. b and c
160. a.
161. d
162. b
163. d
164. b
165. d
166. a
167. d
168. c
169. d
170. d
171. d
172. d

ROBERT ANTON WILSON
Select Bibliography

Fiction

The Sex Magicians (1973)

The Illuminatus Trilogy (collected 1984) w/ Robert Shea
 The Eye in the Pyramid (1975)
 The Golden Apple (1975)
 Leviathan (1975)

Schrödinger's Cat Trilogy (collected and abridged, 1988)
 The Universe Next Door (1979)
 The Trick Top Hat (1981)
 The Homing Pigeons (1981)

Masks of the Illuminati (1981)

The Historical Illuminatus Chronicles
 The Earth Will Shake (1983)
 The Widow's Son (1985)
 Nature's God (1991)

Wilhelm Reich in Hell (1987)

The Walls Came Tumbling Down (1997)

Non-fiction

Playboy's Book of Forbidden Words (1972)

Sex and Drugs: A Journey Beyond Limits (1973)

The Book of the Breast (1974, revised as *Ishtar Rising* 1989)

Cosmic Trigger: The Final Secret of the Illuminati (1977)

Neuropolitics (1978, revised as *Neuropolitique*, 1988) with George A. Koopman and Timothy Leary

The Illuminati Papers (1980)

Right Where You Are Sitting Now (1983)

Prometheus Rising (1983)

The New Inquisition (1986)

Natural Law (1987)

Coincidance: A Head Test (1988)

Quantum Psychology (1990)

Cosmic Trigger Volume II: Down to Earth (1991)

Reality Is What You Can Get Away With (1992)

Chaos and Beyond: The Best of Trajectories (1994) with other contributors

Cosmic Trigger Volume III: My Life After Death (1995)

Everything Is Under Control (1998)

Sex, Drugs & Magick (2000)

TSOG: The Thing that Ate the Constitution (2002)

Email to the Universe (2005)

◆ ◆ ◆